Cooking for Health

Cooking for Health

*Low cholesterol recipes
for weight reduction and heart care*

Helen Ringrose

OMEGA BOOKS

This edition published 1984 by Omega Books Ltd,
1 West Street, Ware, Hertfordshire, under licence
from the proprietor.

Copyright © RPLA Pty Limited 1978

ISBN 0 907853 14 5

Printed and bound in Hong Kong by South China Printing Co.

Previous page: *Lamb Provençal (page 149) and Ratatouille (page 65)*

FOREWORD

If you are overweight and have high levels of blood fats (cholesterol and triglyceride) you increase the risk of suffering from heart disease. This fact is supported by evidence from medical research over the past 15 years. No informed person should willingly run the risk of heart disease by being obese and having high blood-fat levels.

The risk of heart disease can be reduced by following a modified diet. These dietary requirements are well known and relatively simple, but many people find it difficult to implement them. Therefore, a cookbook which incorporates these changes in delicious, simple recipes, is an invaluable aid.

This book provides appetizing, nutritious meals that will satisfy the most demanding of gourmets. But please stick to the rules! The portions specified for each recipe provide gourmet fare with fewer kilojoules (calories) than usual. So do not be tempted by the succulence of the meals to take larger helpings.

Miss Ringrose is a highly qualified dietitian with an international reputation and she is also an excellent cook. Her introduction and comments through the text are in accord with the most recent research into and knowledge of heart disease.

The National Heart Foundation of Australia is very pleased to be associated with Miss Ringrose and the publishers, Paul Hamlyn Pty Limited, in the production of this book, which we believe will make a valuable contribution to the health of the community.

Ralph Reader

Ralph Reader
C.M.G., M.B., B.S. (Syd.), D.Phil. (Oxon), F.R.A.C.P., F.R.C.P.
Director
National Heart Foundation of Australia

CONTENTS

Chicken Salad Mimosa (page 50)

ACKNOWLEDGEMENTS

All the recipes in this book were compiled and tested by consultant dietitians Margaret R. Loucks, D.I.M. (Melb.), Cert. Dietetics (Q.V.H.), and Christine L. Roberts, D.N.F.S. (Melb.), Cert. Dietetics (R.M.H.).

Thanks are also due to the following people for their assistance: Anne Fayle, food for photography; Reg Morrison, photography; Nathalie Quinlivan, B.Sc., Cert. Dietetics, Consultant, National Heart Foundation of Australia; and Pat Ring, manuscript typing.

INTRODUCTION

In the past two decades much has been said about the effect of diet on obesity, blood-fat levels and heart disease. Scientific research the world over has shown that the three conditions are strongly linked. One of the main reasons why we become overweight, and why our blood-fat levels become raised is that we eat the wrong type of foods.

A diet with too many high-energy foods, such as fats, refined carbohydrates, sugars and alcohol, can lead to obesity. Fats, in particular saturated fats and cholesterol, can cause high blood cholesterol levels; and most high-energy foods can lead to high blood triglyceride levels.

We can control several of the risk factors causing heart disease by making modifications to our diet. The recipes in this book are designed to do just that—and in a way that takes none of the pleasure out of eating. This is achieved by keeping fats to a minimum, and, if fats are included, by using as much of the polyunsaturated type as possible. Sugars and refined carbohydrates have also been kept to a minimum.

Throughout the book we will be referring to the energy value of foods in *kilojoules*, a term which has replaced the word *calories*.

If you prepare the recipes regularly, without necessarily counting the kilojoules, they will provide enjoyable meals, and at the same time contribute to a balanced diet, which will assist weight and blood-fat control. If, however, your doctor advises you to adopt an active dietary programme to reduce weight or blood-fat levels, or both, the recipes will provide invaluable help in menu planning. (The approximate calorie or kilojoule count per serve has been calculated for every recipe.)

I have not attempted to provide advice on detailed diets for weight reduction, or for blood-fat reduction—this is a matter for your doctor or dietitian. However, there are several National Heart Foundation publications which set out the principles for dietary modification, which you may wish to read: *Planning Fat-Controlled Meals* and *The Heart Foundation Guide to Losing Weight*.

Helen Ringrose
M.P.H. (Hawaii), D.N.F.S. (Melb.), Cert. Dietetics (R.M.H.), T.T.C.

DIET FOR A HEALTHY HEART

The following general principles have guided the dietitians in the preparation of this book, and we recommend them to you as guidelines for all your food preparation.

Restrict high cholesterol foods
We suggest that you limit serves of red meats to 3 or 4 serves per week. No more than 2 or 3 egg yolks or whole eggs should be eaten per week (this includes eggs used in cookery). For the remaining meals include such protein sources as poultry, fish, veal, low-fat cheeses, nuts, pulses and lentils.

Offal (such as liver, kidney and brains) and all shellfish should be eaten only on special occasions. These foods are among the highest in cholesterol content.

Limit all fats, particularly saturated fats
Most people consume about 40 to 45% of their energy requirements as fat. To help reduce the blood lipids and overall energy intake, we suggest that this percentage be cut down to 35%, with a larger proportion of the fat being consumed as polyunsaturated fats.

A note about polyunsaturated fats—gram for gram, they contain as *many* kilojoules (calories) as saturated fats, and their effect on body weight is the same. It is their effect on blood fats that is different. Therefore, polyunsaturated margarine and oil should replace butter and alternative cooking fats, but should still be used in moderation.

Skim milk, buttermilk, non-fat yoghurts and low-fat cheeses are all acceptable substitutes for whole milk (full cream) products.

Reduce your sugar consumption
Natural sugars are found in fruits, vegetables and 'complex' carbohydrate foods, such as cereals. A well-balanced diet plan can provide adequate sugar for the body's needs from these foods, without using large quantities of refined sugar. Refined sugars and carbohydrates are often referred to as 'empty calorie foods', because they provide energy in a highly concentrated form and very few vitamins and minerals.

Elimination of refined and concentrated sugar products in the diet is, therefore, important for weight control. Avoid the use of sugar in cooking or at the table, and be wary of processed food which lists sugar as one of its major components.

Control your total energy balance
As we become older our physical activity may decline, and with each year our energy requirements may correspondingly decrease to a maintenance level. Unfortunately, many people do not associate their weight problem with the fact that the quantity of food they are eating is greater than their bodily needs.

We know that energy balance is reflected in weight change over the years, and is distinctly related to the major factors which promote accelerated atherosclerosis. Therefore, a combination of exercise and diet must be number-one priority for those wishing to reduce body weight.

To illustrate how your modified fat–modified energy diet can be effective *and* enjoyable, we have planned some sample menus for a basic 5000 kilojoule (1200 calorie) diet. Remember that this diet may not be suitable for everyone, because individual requirements do vary. It would be wise to consult a dietitian before commencing your diet.

In the appendix we have also listed the energy values of some common foods, to help you in planning your own daily diet.

Marinated Mushrooms (page 52)

A Winter Menu

5000 kilojoules (1200 calories)

	Kilojoules[+]	Calories[+]
Breakfast		
Freshly squeezed orange juice—½ cup	220	50
Wholewheat cereal—½ cup	450	110
Skim milk—½ cup	175	40
Savoury Tomatoes*—1 serve	250	60
Toast—1 slice	305	75
Polyunsaturated margarine—1 teaspoon	145	35
Tea or coffee—1 tablespoon skim milk	45	10
Lunch		
Open Danish Sandwich made from:		
Light rye bread—1 slice	220	50
Cottage cheese—1 tablespoon	85	20
Lettuce—1 cup	20	5
Tuna in brine—60 g (2 oz)	320	75
Tomato—½ medium	45	10
Pineapple—1 slice	175	40
Coffee Kosciusko*	340	80
Mid-afternoon		
Mandarin or seasonal fruit—1 serve	225	55
Dinner		
Apricot Fizz*	250	60
Brown Onion Soup*—1 serve	120	30
Lamb Chops Barossa*—1 serve	840	200
Mashed Carrot and Parsnip*—1 serve	190	45
Herbed Chokoes*—1 serve	120	30
Blushing Apples*—1 serve	275	65
Yoghurt Custard*—1 serve	220	50
Tea or coffee—1 tablespoon skim milk	45	10
Approximate number per day	5035	1195

+ Rounded to the nearest 5 kilojoules or calories.
* Recipes included in this book.

A Summer Menu

5000 kilojoules (1200 calories)

	Kilojoules[+]	Calories[+]
Breakfast		
Fresh raspberries—¾ cup	240	50
with		
Non-fat natural yoghurt—½ cup	500	120
Wholemeal toast—1 slice	305	75
Polyunsaturated margarine—1 teaspoon	145	35
Tea or coffee—1 tablespoon skim milk	45	10
Lunch		
Jellied Gazpacho*—1 cup	125	30
Lemon Bream*—1 serve	670	160
Zucchini Salad*—1 serve	150	35
Orange—1 medium	210	50
Tea or coffee—1 tablespoon skim milk	45	10
Mid-afternoon		
Grapefruit juice—½ cup	185	45
Dinner		
Ginger Mint cocktail*	230	55
Chicken Tandoori*—1 serve	1170	280
Cooked rice—½ cup	360	85
Leek and Apple*—1 serve	150	35
Strawberries Flambé*—1 serve	280	70
Whipped Topping*—1 round tablespoon	135	30
Tea or coffee—1 tablespoon skim milk	45	10
Approximate number per day	4980	1190

A NOTE ON POLYUNSATURATED AND LOW-FAT PRODUCTS

A fat-controlled cookbook differs very little from an ordinary cookbook: all we are aiming to do is to limit the amount of ingredients containing cholesterol and saturated fats (such as whole milk, cream, cheese, butter, eggs and fatty meats) so that you may reduce your overall fat intake.

To do this it was necessary for us to devise recipes using low-fat dairy substitutes. Using these outlines as a guide, you too will be able to incorporate fat substitutes quite successfully in your favourite family recipes. Most of these products are 10 to 20% lower in fat content than the normal foods. Thus they are also valuable in reducing the energy content of your diet; but it should be noted that this does not apply to margarine and oils, which have the same energy content as butter.

Polyunsaturated margarine can be used instead of butter in any recipe. Nutritionally, it is the same as butter, but made up of polyunsaturated and monounsaturated oils and fortified with vitamins. Polyunsaturated margarine contains no cholesterol, but must still be used with discretion as it is a concentrated source of kilojoules (calories).

Polyunsaturated oils can successfully replace olive oil, peanut oil, vegetable shortenings, lard and dripping in the frying of foods or preparation of salad dressings. Polyunsaturated oils tend to burn more quickly than other fats, because of their chemical structure. Therefore, it is best to heat oils slowly to begin with, and lower the heat once the oil is at the correct temperature.

Liquid skim milk is now available in cartons, and can be used instead of whole milk in a recipe. A 250 ml cup of skim milk contains only 0.1% fat and less than half the kilojoules (calories), of a cup of whole milk. We suggest you also use it to replace whole milk in tea or coffee, or as a refreshing drink during the day.

Powdered skim milk is slightly more economical than liquid skim milk, and more versatile in food preparation. It is equivalent to liquid skim milk in food value. Do be sure to carefully follow the directions on the packet for reconstitution of powdered milk. Once mixed, store in the refrigerator like fresh milk.

Non-fat natural yoghurts contain no flavours, sweetenings or fruits, and can be incorporated in savoury dishes and sauces where cream is normally used. We recommend stirring the yoghurt to remove lumps before blending into the particular dish. *Never* boil yoghurt or curdling will occur—gentle reheating is all that is required.

Finely diced fresh fruit, fresh herbs, spices, or crisp vegetables stirred through the yoghurt makes an appetizing lunch, and is nutritious and low in kilojoules (calories) too.

Non-fat cottage cheese can be purchased in two forms. 'Curd-style' cottage cheese is creamy in appearance and ideal for dips and snacks. The recipes in this book have all used the curd-style cheese. Commercial varieties include pineapple, gherkin, or chive and onion, in addition to plain cottage cheese. Alternatively, you can create your own nutritious meal by serving cottage cheese accompanied by a fruit or vegetable salad.

Fish Steam Boat (page 84)

Continental-style cottage cheese is also available in a low-fat form. Its smoother consistency enables it to be used in meat dishes, desserts, and as a filling for vegetables.

Buttermilk is made from skim milk with the addition of a lactic acid culture to produce a refreshing, nutritious beverage similar in taste to yoghurt. Buttermilk is a most versatile product because it can be used in sauces and dressings, or as a delicious drink, with the addition of fresh fruit juices. Buttermilk should be refrigerated and stored like fresh milk.

SHOPPING WISELY

The secret of successful low saturated fat–low kilojoule (calorie) cooking lies in the correct selection of foods at the supermarket. To help you purchase the right foods before you start meal preparation, we have compiled a list of suggestions on wise food buying.

Buying meat
- Choice cuts of meat contain considerably more fat (or 'marbling') than the cheaper cuts of meat, and, therefore, should be used sparingly. Veal and lean beef contain less fat than lamb, so they can be used more frequently.
- Chicken and turkey are much lower in saturated fats than red meats, and fish is not only low in saturated fats but low in all fats. These meats and fish should be used whenever possible.
- Do not buy canned, or frozen cooked meat dishes. You have no way of knowing how much fat, or what kinds of fat they contain.
- Limit the use of sausages, luncheon meats (Strasburg, Pork German, luncheon loaf) and meat pastes, as all have a high fat content.
- When buying ground meats, ask your butcher to select lean beef, lamb or veal. Although a little more expensive, this will ensure a minimal fat content. Ready-prepared ground meat can often be 35 to 45% fat. Ground topside is the best choice for beef dishes or hamburgers.
- Always ask your butcher to trim off the excess fat before buying meat. Further trimming may be necessary prior to cooking the meat.

What kind of oil to use
- For both cooking and salad purposes, make sure you buy polyunsaturated vegetable oils. Safflower oil has the highest polyunsaturated content, followed by soybean, sunflower, maize and sesame oils.
- Read the label. It must state that the oil is polyunsaturated. Some oils are blended with saturated vegetable oils, and are therefore unsuitable for use.

Selecting margarines
- Look for the label that states polyunsaturated margarine. There should be a minimum ratio of two parts polyunsaturated to one part saturated vegetable oils.

Orange Borscht (page 38)

- Although margarine is a blend of vegetable oils, if this ratio does not appear on the label, the manufacturing process may have lead to a high saturated fat content. Therefore, labels stating 100% vegetable oil, without giving a polyunsaturated ratio, may be unsuitable.

Milk and dairy products
- A wide variety of low or non-fat dairy products are now available. Skim milk, skim milk powder (instant and regular), buttermilk, non-fat natural yoghurt (containing no sugar or fruit), and non-fat cottage cheese are all low in fat and high in protein, and can be readily substituted for full cream products.
- Beware of imitation creams and toppings. They are usually made from hydrogenated vegetable oils and shortenings which can be quite high in saturated fat content.

Read the label!
- Some manufacturers may list ingredients in descending order of concentration. This can serve as your guide to the contents of the product. Other labels may show ingredients as a percentage of the total product.
- Foods labelled 'dietetic', or 'suitable for diabetics', are not necessarily low in kilojoules (calories), and are not always designed for energy-controlled diets.
- The vast array of 'dietetic' confectionery, biscuits, cakes and ice-creams frequently contain a larger number of kilojoules (calories), and may contain more fat than the products they were designed to replace.

Other commercial products
- Biscuits, cakes, frozen pastry dough, doughnuts and cake mixes may contain eggs, dried egg yolks, whole milk or saturated fats. Unless the label states the type of ingredients, it would be wise to avoid these products.
- Potato crisps, popcorn, pretzels and other snack foods are often cooked in saturated vegetable oils and are not suitable for energy and fat-controlled diets.

METRICS IN THE KITCHEN

All the recipes in this book have been tested using metric measures. For those not yet familiar with metric measures, imperial units of mass, length, volume, calorie value and cooking temperature have also been given.

To ensure consistency when following the recipes, we urge you to purchase a set of metric measures which carry the seal of approval of the Standards Association of Australia.

The set consists of:
- A 250 millilitre (ml) cup for measuring liquids, and a litre measuring jug (capacity 4 cups) with millilitre graduations.
- A set of four measuring cups, based on the 250 ml cup, for measuring dry ingredients. (When using these cups, it is necessary to level off the contents by running a knife across the brim.) The set contains one (full), half, third and quarter cup measures.

- A graduated set of four measuring spoons: tablespoon (20 ml), teaspoon (5 ml), and half and quarter teaspoons. All spoon measurements must be level unless otherwise stated.

Wherever possible, we have tried to give ingredients in cup measurements, rather than by weight. There may be some initial difficulty in estimating the amount of canned or packaged food to purchase, when a recipe calls for a cup of a particular food item. However, as commercial tinned food products vary so greatly in their net contents, we feel that ingredients for recipes can be estimated more accurately if you are guided by cup measures.

Both metric and imperial measures are given in the recipes. However, the following conversion tables may serve as a useful guide.

Oven temperatures

Oven temperatures are expressed in degrees Celsuis (°C) and Fahrenheit (°F) to accommodate new and older ovens. Oven temperatures vary according to make; therefore, the table below gives only a general guide to temperatures of electric ovens. If using a gas oven simply decrease the given temperature by 10°C (25°F).

Description of oven	Celsius °C	Fahrenheit °F
Cool	100	200
Very slow	125	250
Slow	150	300
Moderately slow	160	325
Moderate	180	350
Moderately hot	200	400
Hot	220	425
Very hot	230	450

Mass measures

30 g = 1 oz
60 g = 2 oz
90 g = 3 oz
125 g = 4 oz
155 g = 5 oz
185 g = 6 oz
250 g = 8 oz

315 g = 10 oz
375 g = 12 oz
500 g = 1 lb
750 g = 1½ lb
1 kg = 2 lb
1.2 kg = 2½ lb
1.5 kg = 3 lb

Liquid measures

1 cup = 250 ml
2 cups = 500 ml
4 cups = 1 litre

Abbreviations used

gram g
kilogram kg
millilitre ml
centimetre cm
millimetre mm
kilojoule kJ
ounce oz
pound lb

APPETIZERS

Choosing an appetizer that will delight the eye, stimulate the appetite, and yet not be so high in kilojoules (calories) that the main course must consist of a lettuce leaf is a challenge for any hostess. We have selected the following recipes as examples of dishes that will please everyone, yet allow flexibility in planning the remainder of the meal.

Fresh garden vegetables, fish and fruits form the basis of these appetizers. Most of the ingredients are low in saturated fats, cholesterol and carbohydrates, and can be used to complement many of the meat dishes in the following sections.

So begin your dinner party with Salmon Marguerite or Dolmathes, and sit back and wait for the compliments!

Foreground: *Tuna Tropicana (page 26)*; background: *Salmon Marguerite (page 26)*

Cheese and Pineapple Canapés

Serves: 4   *320 kJ (75 cal) per serve*

4 small starch-reduced rolls
¾ cup non-fat cottage cheese
2 tablespoons finely chopped fresh, or

unsweetened canned pineapple
2 teaspoons finely chopped green ginger
salt

Garnish
16 small pieces dill cucumber
16 small pieces tomato

1 Carefully cut each roll into 4 thin slices, using a serrated knife.
2 Mix cheese with pineapple, ginger and salt, and spread on slices of rolls.
3 Decorate each slice with dill cucumber and tomato.

Celery Sticks

Serves: 4   *190 kJ (45 cal) per serve*

4 stalks celery
½ cup non-fat cottage cheese
2 teaspoons skim milk powder

salt and pepper
1 tablespoon chopped fresh chives

1 Cut celery into 5 cm (2 in) lengths.
2 Blend cheese, skim milk powder, salt and pepper, and purée in a blender or pass through a sieve to make a smooth paste.
3 Add chives.
4 Fill celery sticks with cheese mixture and serve.

Egg Slices and Salmon Canapés

Serves: 4   *260 kJ (60 cal) per serve*

4 small starch-reduced rolls
60 g (2 oz) smoked salmon, thinly sliced

3 eggs, hard-boiled
16 capers

Garnish
parsley, chopped

1 Carefully cut each roll into 4 thin slices using a serrated knife.
2 Cut salmon into 16 even strips and roll up.
3 Peel eggs, slice crosswise and discard yolks.
4 Place one slice of egg white on each slice of roll.
5 Decorate centre of egg slices with salmon and capers.
6 Serve garnished with parsley.

Dolmathes

Serves: 4 (24 dolmathes)
Cooking time: 1 hour
410 kJ (100 cal) per serve

40 preserved vine leaves
2 cooked chicken breasts, skinned and finely chopped
½ cup finely chopped celery
½ cup finely chopped onion
½ cup finely chopped green pepper

½ cup chopped fresh parsley
2 cloves garlic, crushed
juice of ½ lemon
¼ teaspoon mixed dried herbs
salt and pepper
2 tablespoons tomato paste

1 Place vine leaves in a saucepan of cold water. Bring to the boil. Simmer for 5 minutes, pour off the hot water and refill with cold. Stand aside.
2 Mix all other ingredients together.
3 Reserve 24 unbroken leaves.
4 Place remainder of leaves in the bottom of a large saucepan, casserole dish, or baking pan.
5 Place 2 teaspoons of mixture on each reserved leaf. Roll vine leaf around filling, folding in the edges of the leaves. Place dolmathes folded side down in the dish. Pack closely.
6 Add enough cold water to half cover dolmathes. Cover pan tightly.
7 Bring to the boil, reduce heat, and simmer gently for 50 minutes.
8 Allow to cool. Drain off liquid and serve dolmathes on a platter.

Note: Preserved vine leaves can be purchased at continental delicatessens.

Artichoke Hearts Monterey

Serves: 4
320 kJ (75 cal) per serve

1½ cups canned artichoke hearts, drained (approximately 8)
1 cup Buttermilk Dressing (see page 59)

Garnish
parsley sprigs

1 Arrange drained artichoke hearts on 4 individual dishes. Allow 2 per serve.
2 When ready to serve, spoon chilled dressing over artichokes and garnish with parsley sprigs.

Chicken Nibblets

Serves: 6
Oven temperature: 180°C (350°F)

690 kJ (165 cal) per serve

½ **cup soy sauce**
2 **cloves garlic, crushed**
1 **medium onion, roughly chopped**
2 **teaspoons grated green ginger**
2 **tablespoons chopped fresh chives**

salt and pepper
4 **drops artificial liquid sweetener**
4 **tablespoons dry sherry**
1 **tablespoon polyunsaturated oil**
1.5 **kg (3 lb) chicken wings**

Garnish
parsley, chopped

1 In a mixing bowl, combine all ingredients, except chicken.
2 Wash and dry chicken wings.
3 Cut off the wing tips at the joint.
4 Remove the thinner bone from the wing. Scrape down the chicken flesh on the remaining bone to the end to make a drumstick shape.
5 Add the chicken to the marinade. Cover and refrigerate for 2 hours, stirring occasionally.
6 Place chicken in a baking pan. Strain marinade over chicken and bake in the oven at 180°C (350°F) for 30 minutes or until tender, basting occasionally with marinade.
7 Remove chicken from pan and brush with pan juices. Serve on a platter, sprinkle with parsley.

Stuffed Tomatoes

Serves: 4

630 kJ (150 cal) per serve

4 **large, firm tomatoes**
¾ **cup chunk-style tuna, in brine, drained**
juice of ½ lemon
¾ **cup non-fat cottage cheese**

1 **tablespoon chopped fresh parsley**
salt and pepper
garlic salt to taste
4 **cup-shaped lettuce leaves**

1 Slice off the tops of tomatoes and reserve, scoop out the pulp. Reserve the firm flesh of 2 tomatoes. Discard the remainder.
2 Mix drained fish, lemon juice, cottage cheese, parsley and seasoning.
3 Fill tomatoes with this mixture and replace the tops.
4 Arrange tomatoes on lettuce leaves. Serve chilled.

Salmon Marguerite

Serves: 4   *440 kJ (105 cal) per serve*

155 g (5 oz) smoked salmon, finely
  chopped
¼ cup finely chopped spring onions
  or shallots
¼ cup finely chopped celery

¼ teaspoon dried dill
¾ cup non-fat natural yoghurt
2 tablespoons prepared horseradish sauce
salt and pepper
4 cup-shaped lettuce leaves

Garnish

1 teaspoon smoked salmon, chopped or
  cut into strips

1   Combine salmon, spring onions, celery and dill.
2   In a separate bowl, combine yoghurt, horseradish, salt and pepper.
3   Season yoghurt dressing with salt and pepper. Add extra horseradish, if
    necessary.
4   Combine yoghurt dressing with salmon mixture. Toss gently.
5   Serve on lettuce leaves. Garnish with smoked salmon pieces.

Tuna Tropicana

Serves: 4   *740 kJ (175 cal) per serve*

1 small pineapple
¾ cup chunk-style tuna, in brine, drained
1 cup sliced strawberries
1 cup cubed cantaloup (rock melon)

2 tablespoons lemon juice
¼ cup unsweetened pineapple juice
4 drops artificial liquid sweetener

Garnish

¼ cup non-fat natural yoghurt
4 whole strawberries (extra)

1   Cut pineapple lengthwise into quarters through green top.
2   Remove flesh from quarters. Dry skins with a paper towel.
3   Cut flesh of 2 quarters into chunks, store remainder for use on another
    occasion.
4   Place pineapple chunks, tuna, strawberries, and cantaloup (rock melon) in a
    large bowl. Sprinkle with lemon juice, pineapple juice and sweetener. Toss,
    then refrigerate for 1 hour.
5   Spoon mixture into shells.
6   Spoon 1 tablespoon yoghurt on each serve. Garnish with extra strawberries.

Herring Rollups

Serves: 4   *740 kJ (175 cal) per serve*

1 medium apple, cored and diced
½ cup finely chopped celery
¼ cup finely chopped onion
¼ cup chopped walnuts
1 tablespoon chopped fresh parsley

2-3 drops artificial liquid sweetener
1 tablespoon lemon juice
½ cup non-fat natural yoghurt
4 herring rollmops
4 cup-shaped lettuce leaves

Garnish
red pepper (capsicum) or pimento strips
parsley, chopped

1   Combine apple, celery, onion, walnuts, parsley, sweetener and lemon juice with yoghurt.
2   Unroll herrings, place 2 tablespoons mixture on each. Re-roll.
3   Place rollmops on lettuce leaves.
4   Place 1 teaspoon of mixture beside each rollmop. Chill well.
5   Garnish with red pepper (capsicum) or pimento strips and chopped parsley.

Frogs' Legs Meunière

Serves: 4   *760 kJ (180 cal) per serve*
Cooking time: 15 minutes

4 pairs frogs' legs
2 cups skim milk or beer
2 tablespoons polyunsaturated oil
1 clove garlic, crushed

1 tablespoon lemon juice
salt
black pepper, freshly ground

Garnish
2 tablespoons chopped fresh parsley
8 cucumber slices
4 tomato wedges

1   If legs are large, split pairs at the top.
2   Soak legs in skim milk or beer for 2 hours, drain and dry.
3   Heat oil in a flat pan with garlic.
4   Sauté legs until golden (approximately 2½ minutes on each side).
5   Season with lemon juice, salt and pepper.
6   If legs are large, cover and cook for a further 10 minutes or until tender.
7   Sprinkle with chopped parsley, and serve hot with a garnish of cucumber and tomato.

Note: Frogs' legs can be purchased frozen or tinned at gourmet delicatessens.

Stuffed Artichokes

Serves: 4
Cooking time: 40 minutes
Oven temperature 220°C (425°F)

680 kJ (165 cal) per serve

4 fresh globe artichokes
juice of 2 lemons
1 cup non-fat cottage cheese
1 clove garlic, crushed
1 tablespoon finely chopped capers

2 tablespoons finely chopped parsley
salt
black pepper, freshly ground
1 tablespoon polyunsaturated oil

1 Cut off the stems of artichokes, remove 4-5 coarse outer leaves, and trim the remaining leaves. Scoop out the choke (the inner fibrous core).
2 Drop artichokes into boiling, salted water, adding half of the lemon juice. Cook for 10 minutes.
3 Drain, rinse in cold water, and set aside.
4 For filling, thoroughly blend the cottage cheese and all other ingredients except oil.
5 Gently open the leaves.
6 Stuff each artichoke with the filling and place into a shallow baking dish.
7 Rub each artichoke with a little oil and remaining lemon juice, cover the dish and bake in the oven at 220°C (425°F) for 30 minutes.
8 Serve hot.

Mushroom Soufflé

Serves: 4

175 kJ (40 cal) per serve

125 g (4 oz) fresh mushrooms, sliced
2 tablespoons skim milk powder
4 tablespoons water
8 drops yellow food colouring

¼ teaspoon salt
pinch pepper
¼ teaspoon polyunsaturated oil
4 egg whites

Garnish
2 teaspoons finely chopped fresh parsley

1 Simmer mushrooms in a little water until tender. Set aside.
2 Blend skim milk powder with water and add yellow colouring, salt and pepper.
3 Rub a well-seasoned or non-stick 25 cm (10 in) frying pan with oil and place on a hotplate to heat.
4 Beat egg whites until stiff.
5 Gently fold skim milk mixture into egg whites.
6 Place in the pan and cook until the base of the mixture is set.
7 Place mushrooms on top of egg mixture and grill until mixture begins to brown.
8 Sprinkle with parsley. Cut soufflé into 4 pieces and serve immediately.

Curried Eggs

Serves: 6   *150 kJ (35 cal) per serve*

6 eggs, hard-boiled
½ cup non-fat cottage cheese
2 teaspoons skim milk powder

1 teaspoon curry powder
salt and pepper
8 drops yellow food colouring

Garnish
12 small sprigs parsley

1. Peel eggs and cut in half, lengthwise.
2. Scrape out yolks and discard.
3. Blend cheese, skim milk powder, curry powder, salt, pepper and colouring together. Purée in a blender or pass through a sieve to make a smooth paste.
4. Pipe or spoon cheese mixture into egg whites and top each with a small sprig of parsley.

Fennel à La Grecque

Serves: 4   *135 kJ (30 cal) per serve*
Cooking time: 20 minutes

2 fennel bulbs
rind of 1 lemon, grated
½ teaspoon chopped fresh thyme, or
pinch dried thyme
1 bay leaf

4 tablespoons tomato paste
3 cups dry white wine
salt
black pepper, freshly ground
¼ teaspoon ground coriander

1. Trim and wash fennel bulbs, and cut each lengthwise into 6 even pieces.
2. Place pieces of fennel in a saucepan, and add lemon rind, thyme, bay leaf, tomato paste, wine, salt, pepper and coriander.
3. Simmer over a low heat until tender (approximately 30 minutes).
4. Carefully lift out fennel and place into a deep serving dish.
5. Strain the cooking liquid and reduce over a high heat to half the volume.
6. Pour the liquid over fennel.
7. Serve chilled — three pieces to a serve.

Stuffed Leeks

Serves: 4   *285 kJ (70 cal) per serve*
Cooking time: 40 minutes
Oven temperature: 180°C (350°F)

6 leeks   salt
½ cup non-fat cottage cheese   pinch nutmeg
½ cup finely diced tomato   pinch cayenne pepper
1 clove garlic, crushed   ½ cup water
1 tablespoon chopped fresh parsley

1   Trim leeks by cutting off green leaves and roots.
2   Cut each leek into pieces 6 cm (2½ in) long. Wash thoroughly.
3   Blanch in boiling, salted water for 8-10 minutes, and drain well.
4   With an apple corer, remove centre of each piece of leek.
5   Blend cheese, tomato, garlic, parsley, salt, nutmeg and cayenne pepper together, and fill each piece of leek with this mixture.
6   Place in a baking dish with water, and cover with a tight-fitting lid or aluminium foil.
7   Cook in the oven at 180°C (350°F) for 30 minutes.
8   Chill well before serving.

Beef and Asparagus Rolls

Serves: 4   *560 kJ (135 cal) per serve*

1 x 440 g (15 oz) can of large asparagus   12 wooden toothpicks
  spears
185 g (6 oz) cooked corned beef, thinly
  sliced

Garnish
4 large sprigs of parsley

1   Drain asparagus spears.
2   Trim meat into 7 cm (2¾ in) squares, and remove all visible fat.
3   Lay one asparagus spear diagonally across each square of meat, roll up and secure with a toothpick.
4   Serve cold, garnished with sprigs of parsley.

Grapefruit Cups

Serves: 4   *225 kJ (55 cal) per serve*

2 large grapefruit   4 cup-shaped lettuce leaves
1 quantity of Cocktail Sauce (see page 61)

1   Halve grapefruit and cut around the fruit between the skin and flesh with a sharp knife.
2   Remove the flesh, discarding any membrane and pith, and cut into 10 mm (½ in) pieces.
3   Mix with cocktail sauce, cover and chill.
4   Line grapefruit skins with lettuce, fill with grapefruit mixture and serve.

Minted Pineapple

Serves: 4   *190 kJ (45 cal) per serve*

1½ cups diced fresh pineapple or 2 cups   1 tablespoon finely chopped fresh mint
  unsweetened canned pineapple   ½ cup fresh orange juice

Garnish
4 sprigs mint

1 Place pineapple in a basin.
2 Add chopped mint and orange juice and stir well.
3 Cover bowl and chill well.
4 Serve in cocktail glasses and garnish each with sprig of mint.

Asparagus Tartare

Serves: 4   *270 kJ (65 cal) per serve*

750 g (1½ lb) fresh asparagus   1 cup Tartare Sauce (see page 61)
4 lettuce leaves

1 Wash asparagus, snap off woody end and scrape white part with a knife to remove outer layer of stalk.
2 Place asparagus into boiling, salted water and cook until tender (approximately 10 minutes).
3 Drain and chill well.
4 Arrange on lettuce leaves and serve on a flat dish with tartare sauce served to one side.

SOUPS

The good thing about soup is that it is economical, simple to prepare, nutritious, and usually low in kilojoules (calories), fats and cholesterol.

A well-flavoured stock is essential for a tasty soup. Therefore, we have included instructions for the preparation of beef, chicken and fish stocks, which can be used for soups, sauces, gravies and meat dishes.

Here are some useful cooking tips for preparing low-fat soups:

- Prepare the stock the day before use and stand it overnight in the refrigerator. The solid fat that accumulates can then be removed easily prior to cooking. Stock itself is a nutritious, low kilojoule (calorie) beverage that can be included freely in most diets.

- Commercial stock cubes and granules can be substituted for home-made stocks if time is short. We suggest that you have a variety of stock flavours on hand for that meal-in-a-minute.

- Home-made stock can be frozen and used as required. Two cups of stock should be sufficient for most recipes. Measure out and freeze this amount in separate plastic containers.

- Replace some of the cooking liquid in your favourite soup with half a cup of white wine. Wine imparts a delicious flavour and does not add any extra kilojoules (calories) after it is boiled.

Iced Fruit Soup (page 43)

Tarator Soup

Serves: 4   *670 kJ (160 cal) per serve*

1 large cucumber, peeled and grated
salt
1 large green pepper (capsicum) grated
2 cups non-fat natural yoghurt
½ cup finely chopped walnuts

2 cloves garlic, crushed
2 tablespoons lemon juice
2 drops green food colouring
black pepper

Garnish
fresh or dried dill

1 Sprinkle grated cucumber with salt. Refrigerate for 1 hour.
2 Combine green pepper (capsicum) and yoghurt in a large bowl.
3 Add walnuts, garlic, lemon juice, colouring and pepper to taste.
4 Add cucumber. Check flavour and adjust seasonings to taste.
5 Chill in the refrigerator for 2 hours.
6 Serve garnished with a sprinkle of fresh or dried dill.

Iced Tomato Soup

Serves: 4   *355 kJ (85 cal) per serve*

3 cups unsweetened tomato juice
1 cup non-fat natural yoghurt
1 cup peeled and finely diced cucumber
grated rind of 1 lemon

grated rind of 1 orange
½ small onion, finely chopped
2 teaspoons chopped fresh chives
salt and pepper (optional)

Garnish
1 teaspoon finely chopped fresh mint

1 Combine tomato juice and yoghurt in a large bowl.
2 Beat with an electric or hand beater until well mixed.
3 Add cucumber, lemon rind, orange rind, onion and chives.
4 Check flavour, add salt and pepper if required.
5 Chill for 2 hours in the refrigerator.
6 Serve sprinkled with fresh mint.

Fish Soup

Serves: 4   *200 kJ (50 cal) per serve*
Cooking time: 5 minutes

250 g (8 oz) white fish fillets

1 quantity Court Bouillon (see page 45)

Garnish
1 teaspoon finely chopped fresh parsley

1 Finely slice fish fillets.
2 Bring Court Bouillon to the boil.
3 Drop fish slices into the liquid and simmer gently for 3 minutes.
4 Serve hot with a sprinkling of parsley.

Brown Onion Soup

Serves: 4
Cooking time: 30 minutes

130 kJ (30 cal) per serve

1 medium brown onion, sliced
2 teaspoons polyunsaturated oil

4 cups Basic Meat Stock (see page 45)

1 Place onion in a saucepan with oil.
2 Stir over a high heat until the onions are well browned.
3 Add the stock and simmer for 30 minutes.
4 Serve hot.

Egg and Green Pea Soup

Serves: 4
Cooking time: 8-10 minutes

160 kJ (40 cal) per serve

4 cups Chicken Stock (see page 45)
125 g (4 oz) peas
1 teaspoon finely chopped green ginger
1 teaspoon brandy

¼ teaspoon monosodium glutamate
8 spring onions, chopped
2 egg whites

1 Bring stock to the boil.
2 Add peas, ginger, brandy and monosodium glutamate, simmer for 8-10 minutes or until peas are tender.
3 Add spring onions.
4 Gently beat egg whites with a fork (avoid creating too much froth).
5 Remove the saucepan from the hotplate.
6 Add the egg whites slowly, stirring the soup gently. Serve hot.

Cream of Asparagus Soup

Serves: 4
Cooking time: 20 minutes

500 kJ (120 cal) per serve

3 cups canned green asparagus spears, drained and chopped (reserve juice)
2 teaspoons dry sherry
pinch nutmeg

pepper and salt to taste
2 cups Double-Strength Skim Milk (see page 44)

Garnish
reserved asparagus tips

1 Place asparagus juice in a saucepan.
2 Reserve some asparagus tips for the garnish.
3 Add asparagus, sherry, nutmeg, pepper and salt to liquid.
4 Bring to the boil, simmer gently for 10 minutes.
5 Add milk, reheat just to boiling point.
6 Check flavour and serve, garnished with asparagus tips.

Leek Soup

Serves: 4
Cooking time: 15 minutes

425 kJ (100 cal) per serve

4 cups Basic Meat Stock (see page 45)
1 cup cooked meat used in preparation
  of stock

1 large leek
salt

1 Pour stock into a saucepan.
2 Remove all visible fat from meat, dice and add to stock.
3 Finely slice leek, discarding roots and coarse parts of leaves, and wash well.
4 Bring stock to the boil, add leeks and salt and simmer for 15 minutes.
5 Serve hot.

Spinach Soup

Serves: 4
Cooking time: 5 minutes

60 kJ (15 cal) per serve

4 cups Basic Meat Stock (see page 45)
2 teaspoons soy sauce
125 g (4 oz) spinach leaves, with stalks
  removed

2 egg whites

1 Combine stock and soy sauce in a saucepan, and bring to the boil.
2 Wash, drain and finely shred the spinach.
3 Add to the stock and boil for 3-5 minutes until leaves are just tender.
4 Gently beat the egg whites with a fork (avoid creating too much froth).
5 Remove the saucepan from the hotplate.
6 Add the egg whites slowly, stirring the soup gently. Serve hot.

Tomato Soup

Serves: 4
Cooking time: 40 minutes

195 kJ (45 cal) per serve

500 g (1 lb) fresh tomatoes, chopped
2 cups water
2 chicken stock cubes
1 teaspoon salt
1 medium onion, chopped roughly

1 bay leaf
pinch mixed dried herbs
4 tablespoons tomato paste
8-12 drops artificial liquid sweetener
salt and pepper (optional)

Garnish
rind of 1 orange, grated

1 Place tomatoes in a large saucepan.
2 Add water, stock cubes, salt, onion, bay leaf and herbs.
3 Bring slowly to the boil. Reduce heat and simmer gently for 30 minutes.
4 Remove bay leaf and purée liquid in a blender or rub through a sieve. Return liquid to the saucepan.
5 Add tomato paste, sweetener, pepper and salt.
6 Bring to the boil and serve.
7 Garnish with a sprinkle of orange rind.

Chicken Gumbo

Serves: 6
Cooking time: 45 minutes

420 kJ (100 cal) per serve

1 tablespoon polyunsaturated margarine
1 cup chopped celery
1 cup chopped green pepper (capsicum)
1 medium onion, chopped
3 cups Chicken Stock (see page 45)
½ cup canned or fresh okra, sliced into rings

1 cup chopped cooked chicken
1 cup chopped fresh or canned tomatoes
black pepper
salt
pinch mixed dried herbs
½ cup unsweetened tomato juice

Garnish
parsley, chopped

1   Melt margarine in a large pan, add celery, green pepper (capsicum) and onion. Fry until soft.
2   Add chicken stock and bring to the boil. Simmer for 10 minutes.
3   Add okra, chicken, tomatoes, seasonings and tomato juice.
4   Return to the boil, simmer for 30 minutes.
5   Check seasoning.
6   Serve garnished with chopped parsley.

Orange Borscht

Serves: 4
Cooking time: 30 minutes

420 kJ (100 cal) per serve

3 cups peeled and grated raw beetroot
4 cups Basic Meat Stock (see page 45)
1½ cups unsweetened tomato juice
1 teaspoon salt

½ teaspoon dried thyme
¼ teaspoon black pepper
1 cup unsweetened orange juice

Garnish
4 teaspoons non-fat natural yoghurt
fresh chives or parsley, chopped

1   Place beetroot and stock in a saucepan.
2   Bring to the boil. Simmer for 20 minutes or until tender.
3   Strain the broth. Return 1 cup beetroot to broth. Discard the remainder.
4   Add tomato juice, salt, thyme and pepper. Bring to the boil.
5   Add orange juice and reheat.
6   Serve garnished with yoghurt, and chives or parsley.

Asparagus and Chicken Soup

Serves: 4
Cooking time: 35-45 minutes

610 kJ (145 cal) per serve

2 chicken breasts
2 cups canned asparagus cuts
water
salt

¼ teaspoon monosodium glutamate
1 teaspoon brandy
¼ cup skim milk powder, dissolved in ½
cup cold water

Garnish
1 teaspoon finely chopped fresh parsley

1 Slice the chicken meat into thin strips approximately 2½ cm (1 in) long.
2 Drain asparagus and retain juice in a saucepan.
3 Add water to juice to make a total of 4 cups of liquid.
4 Add chicken and salt to liquid.
5 Bring to the boil and simmer for approximately 30-40 minutes or until chicken is tender.
6 Add asparagus pieces, monosodium glutamate and brandy.
7 Simmer for a further 5 minutes.
8 Add skim milk mixture, check flavour and add more salt if necessary.
9 Reheat and serve hot with a sprinkling of chopped parsley.

Rich Carrot Soup

Serves: 4
Cooking time: 30 minutes

610 kJ (145 cal) per serve

500 g (1 lb) carrots, roughly chopped
2 cups water
2 cups Double-Strength Skim Milk (see
page 44)

salt
1 teaspoon curry powder
½ cup chopped fresh parsley

1 Boil carrots in 2 cups water for approximately 20 minutes or until tender.
2 Purée in a blender or rub through a sieve. Return carrot liquid to the saucepan.
3 Add milk, salt, curry powder and parsley.
4 Bring to the boil and serve.

Cool Cucumber Soup

Serves: 4
Cooking time: 20 minutes

120 kJ (30 cal) per serve

4 cups boiling water
4 chicken stock cubes
1 large onion, chopped
2 large cucumbers, peeled and finely chopped (reserve 2 tablespoons for garnish)

1 teaspoon finely chopped fresh mint
salt and pepper
4 drops green food colouring

Garnish
2 tablespoons chopped cucumber
4 mint sprigs

1 Pour boiling water over stock cubes in a saucepan.
2 Add onion and bring to the boil. Simmer for 10 minutes or until onion is soft.
3 Add cucumber and mint, and simmer a further 10 minutes.
4 Purée in a blender or rub through a sieve into a large bowl.
5 Flavour with salt and pepper.
6 Add green colouring.
7 Chill in the refrigerator for at least 4 hours.
8 Serve, garnished with cucumber and mint sprigs.

Bean Shoot Soup

Serves: 4
Cooking time: 40-50 minutes

390 kJ (90 cal) per serve

2 chicken breasts
4 cups water
salt

185 g (6 oz) bean shoots
2 teaspoons soy sauce
8 spring onions or shallots, chopped

1 Dice chicken meat.
2 Place meat in a saucepan with water and salt to taste.
3 Bring to the boil and simmer for 30-40 minutes, until chicken is tender.
4 Wash and drain bean shoots, add to chicken, and simmer for a further 8 minutes.
5 Add soy sauce and spring onions. Serve hot.

Lamb Shank Soup

Serves: 4
Cooking time: 3½ hours

390 kJ (90 cal) per serve

2 lamb shanks, trimmed of all visible fat
6 cups cold water
2 teaspoons salt
2 beef stock cubes
½ large or 1 medium carrot, grated

2 stalks celery, chopped finely
1 large onion, chopped finely
2 tablespoons chopped fresh parsley
salt and pepper

1 Place shanks, water and salt in a large saucepan and bring slowly to the boil.
2 Reduce heat and simmer until shanks are tender (about 3 hours).
3 Allow to cool. Skim off any fat from soup.
4 Remove shanks, trim off any gristle and skin and discard. Chop meat finely, and return to soup.
5 Add stock cubes and vegetables to soup.
6 Bring soup to the boil and simmer gently until vegetables are cooked.
7 Check flavour. Add parsley, salt and pepper before serving.

Iced Fruit Soup

Serves: 4
Cooking time: 15-20 minutes

555 kJ (130 cal) per serve

500 g (1 lb) cooking apples, peeled, cored and sliced
1 punnet strawberries, washed and hulled (reserve 4 for garnish)
2 cups unsweetened tinned apricots, drained
2 cups fresh or frozen raspberries or blackberries

¼ teaspoon cinnamon
grated rind and juice of 1 lemon
¾ cup cold water
½ cup unsweetened orange juice
½ cup unsweetened pineapple juice
½ teaspoon artificial liquid sweetener

Garnish
¼ cup non-fat natural yoghurt
4 strawberries, sliced

1 Place fruit, lemon rind, lemon juice, cinnamon and water in a saucepan.
2 Bring to the boil, reduce heat and simmer for about 15-20 minutes or until fruit is soft.
3 Purée fruit in an electric blender or rub through a wire sieve. Pour liquid into a large bowl and allow to cool.
4 Add orange juice, pineapple juice, and artificial liquid sweetener. Check flavour and add more sweetener if desired.
5 Chill well in the refrigerator.
6 Serve in glass dishes. Garnish each with a spoonful of yoghurt and 1 sliced strawberry.

Meat Ball Soup

Serves: 6
Cooking time: 15 minutes

650 kJ (155 cal) per serve

6 cups water
3 tablespoons tomato paste
1 medium carrot, diced
1 small green pepper (capsicum), diced
salt
500 g (1 lb) lean topside, finely minced

1 small onion, finely chopped
1 egg white
salt and pepper
pinch mixed dried herbs
1 cup broccoli flowerettes

1 Place water in a saucepan with tomato paste, carrot, green pepper and salt. Bring to the boil, simmer gently.
2 Mix meat with onion, egg white, salt, pepper and herbs.
3 Roll mixture into small balls of about 1 teaspoon each.
4 Drop into boiling stock and simmer for 10 minutes.
5 Add broccoli and simmer for a further 5 minutes.
6 Cool soup and store in the refrigerator overnight.
7 Remove fat, reheat and serve hot.

Cream of Pumpkin Soup

Serves: 4
Cooking time: 30-40 minutes

355 kJ (85 cal) per serve

4 cups Basic Meat Stock (see page 45)
375 g (12 oz) pumpkin, peeled, seeded and chopped

¼ cup skim milk powder
½ cup cold water
salt

Garnish
1 teaspoon finely chopped fresh parsley

1 Place stock and pumpkin into a saucepan.
2 Bring to the boil.
3 Simmer for 30-40 minutes or until pumpkin is soft.
4 Mix skim milk powder with cold water, stirring to dissolve lumps.
5 Combine pumpkin, milk and salt.
6 Purée all ingredients in a blender, or pass through a wire sieve until smooth.
7 Pour back into the saucepan and reheat.
8 Serve hot with a sprinkling of parsley.

Double-Strength Skim Milk

cold water
125 g (4 oz) non-fat milk powder

1 Add sufficient cold water to milk powder to make 600 ml (1 pint) of liquid.
2 Mix until powder has dissolved.

Basic Meat Stock

Yield: 1.5 litres (3 pints)
Cooking time: 3 hours

2 lamb shanks or 500 g (1 lb) gravy beef
2 litres (4 pints) water
1 large carrot
1 medium parsnip
2 stalks celery

2 medium onions
2 teaspoons salt
pinch pepper
pinch mixed dried herbs
1 bay leaf

1   Place meat and cold water in a large saucepan.
2   Chop vegetables into chunks and add to the saucepan with salt, pepper and herbs.
3   Bring slowly to the boil. Reduce heat and simmer gently for 3 hours.
4   Strain through a sieve. Discard bones and vegetables. Refrigerate stock.
5   Remove all visible fat before use.

Court Bouillon

Yield: 1 litre (2 pints)
Serves: 4
Cooking time: 30 minutes

500 g (1 lb) fish trimmings
3 cups water
3 cups white wine
1 small carrot, roughly chopped
1 small white onion, roughly chopped

4 peppercorns
1 bouquet garni (of parsley, bay leaf
   and thyme)
salt

1   Place fish trimmings, water, wine, carrot, onion, peppercorns, bouquet garni and salt into a saucepan and cook gently for 30 minutes.
2   Strain and use as required.

Chicken Stock

Yield: 1½ litres (3 pints)
Cooking time: 3 hours

1 x No.15 (1.5 kg) boiling fowl
1 large onion, roughly chopped
1 large carrot, roughly chopped
1 stalk celery, roughly chopped
8 peppercorns

1 bay leaf
pinch dried thyme
5 sprigs parsley
2 teaspoons salt
2 litres (4 pints) water

1   Place all ingredients into a large saucepan. Add cold water.
2   Bring slowly to the boil. Reduce heat and simmer gently for 3 hours.
3   Strain through a sieve. Discard bones and vegetables.
4   Refrigerate stock. Remove all visible fat before use.

SALADS AND SALAD DRESSINGS

Salads are the dieter's best friend. Whether served as a side salad or as a separate dish before or after the main course, salads are generally high in fibre, vitamins and minerals, and low in kilojoules (calories), saturated fats and cholesterol.

A salad tastes even more delicious when accompanied by a tasty dressing, so try some of the salad dressings at the end of this chapter. To ensure that the correct quantity of dressing is served, allow approximately one tablespoon of dressing per serve; most recipes will yield 12 serves per cup.

To help you prepare the perfect salad we suggest you follow these simple rules of salad making:

- Chill the salad plates or bowl before serving the salad.
- Use salad greens that are fresh, crisp, clean, cold and dry.
- Thoroughly rinse all salad greens and gently pat dry with a towel. Store greens in the refrigerator until ready for use.
- Add colour and texture contrasts by combining two or three different salad greens in your next tossed salad.
- Toss the salad just before serving the meal, or prepare salads in individual glass dishes and serve the dressing separately.
- Use finely chopped fresh herbs liberally. Dried herbs can be substituted, but they should be crushed first to release the full flavour.

Foreground: *Orange Fantasia (page 54)*; background: *Neptune Salad (page 50), Creamy Orange Dressing (page 60)*

47

Jellied Gazpacho

Serves: 8   125 kJ (30 cal) per serve
Cooking time: 4 minutes

2 cups unsweetened tomato juice   2 tomatoes, finely chopped
1 beef stock cube   ½ medium onion, finely chopped
3 teaspoons gelatine   ¼ cup finely chopped celery
2 tablespoons vinegar   ½ cup peeled and diced cucumber
salt and pepper   2 tablespoons chopped fresh parsley

Garnish
mint sprigs

1   Pour tomato juice into a saucepan. Add crumbled stock cube.
2   Sprinkle gelatine over mixture and heat until gelatine is dissolved.
3   Add vinegar, salt and pepper, and pour into a decorative mould. Refrigerate
    until beginning to thicken.
4   Carefully fold in vegetables and parsley. Refrigerate until set.
5   When set, turn out by plunging mould into hot water and inverting onto a
    serving plate.
6   Decorate with mint sprigs.

Spinach Valentino

Serves: 4   250 kJ (60 cal) per serve

1 bunch spinach   1 clove garlic, crushed
2 eggs, hard-boiled   salt and pepper
125 g (4 oz) fresh mushrooms, sliced   2 spring onions, sliced
Dressing
¼ cup unsweetened orange juice
1 tablespoon soy sauce
1 teaspoon polyunsaturated oil

1   Thoroughly wash spinach leaves, remove stalks. Pat leaves dry with kitchen
    paper, tear spinach into bite-size pieces.
2   Peel eggs, cut in half lengthwise, discard yolks. Cut egg whites into lengthwise
    strips.
3   Combine spinach, mushrooms and egg whites in a serving bowl with garlic,
    salt, pepper and spring onions.
4   Blend dressing ingredients and pour over salad. Chill before serving.

Salad Florentine

Serves: 4   90 kJ (20 cal) per serve

1 medium green pepper (capsicum), diced   1 medium tomato, diced
1 medium red pepper (capsicum), diced   ¼ quantity Italian Dressing (see page 59)

1   Combine all ingredients.
2   Chill for 1 hour prior to serving.

From left to right: *Herbed Tomato Dressing (page 60), Buttermilk Dressing (page
                          59), Italian Dressing (page 59)*

Chicken Salad Mimosa

Serves: 4   *915 kJ (220 cal) per serve*

2 cups cooked and diced chicken meat
1 cup diced celery
2 hard-boiled egg whites, chopped
1 small green pepper (capsicum), chopped
1 small red pepper (capsicum), chopped
4 spring onions, chopped

2 tomatoes, chopped
1 tablespoon chopped fresh parsley
salt
black pepper
4 cup-shaped lettuce leaves

Dressing
¾ cup non-fat natural yoghurt
2 tablespoons vinegar
½ teaspoon dry mustard

black pepper
2 drops yellow food colouring
salt

Garnish
8 asparagus spears

1   Combine diced chicken with celery, egg whites, peppers, onions, tomatoes, parsley, salt and pepper.
2   Blend dressing ingredients. Add to chicken mixture. Refrigerate for 1 hour.
3   Spoon on to lettuce leaves. Garnish with asparagus spears.

Neptune Salad

Serves: 6   *735 kJ (175 cal) per serve*
Cooking time: 5 minutes

1st Layer
1 cup unsweetened tomato juice
salt and pepper

3 teaspoons Worcestershire sauce
1 teaspoon gelatine

2nd Layer
1 cup non-fat cottage cheese
¾ cup non-fat natural yoghurt
2 tablespoons lemon juice
grated rind of 1 lemon
1 cup red salmon
1 cup tuna (in brine)

4 spring onions, sliced
1 cup chopped celery
½ teaspoon garlic salt
pepper
2 teaspoons gelatine

Garnish
tomato wedges
parsley sprigs

1   Combine tomato juice, salt, pepper, Worcestershire sauce and gelatine in a saucepan. Heat until gelatine has dissolved.
2   Pour into a slightly wet, decorative mould. Refrigerate until set.
3   Mix cottage cheese with an electric beater until smooth and creamy. Purée in a blender or rub through a wire sieve to remove lumps. Add yoghurt, lemon juice and rind.
4   Drain fish, removing any bones and skin. Stir into cheese mixture. Add onions, celery, garlic salt and pepper.
5   Dissolve gelatine in 1 tablespoon hot water. Cool slightly and stir into cheese. Pour into mould. Refrigerate until set (about 2 hours).
6   Turn out by plunging mould into hot water and inverting onto a serving plate. Garnish with tomato and parsley.

Carrot Slaw

Serves: 6   *205 kJ (50 cal) per serve*

3 cups finely shredded cabbage
1 cup grated carrot
2 tablespoons chopped fresh parsley

1 onion, finely chopped
1 stalk celery, finely chopped
grated rind of 1 orange

Dressing
½ cup buttermilk
1 tablespoon prepared horseradish sauce

salt
black pepper, freshly ground

1 Combine cabbage, carrot, parsley, onion, celery and orange rind in a salad bowl.
2 Blend dressing ingredients together.
3 Pour dressing over salad, toss lightly. Chill until required.

Coleslaw

Serves: 4   *295 kJ (70 cal) per serve*

½ medium cabbage
1 large onion, grated
1 green pepper (capsicum), finely chopped
3 stalks celery, finely chopped

1 cup grated carrot
black pepper
1 teaspoon garlic salt
2 cloves garlic, crushed
1 quantity Yoghurt Dressing (see page 59)

1 Remove hard centre core from cabbage.
2 Shred cabbage finely, removing any tough stalks.
3 Toss all ingredients in a large salad bowl.
4 Pour dressing over slaw, chill until ready to serve.

Artichoke Hearts and Asparagus Salad

Serves: 6   *120 kJ (30 cal) per serve*
Cooking time: 35 minutes

6 fresh artichokes
juice of 1 lemon

500 g (1 lb) fresh asparagus
1 quantity French Dressing (see page 60)

1 Cut off stems of artichokes, remove 4 or 5 coarse outer leaves, and trim the sharp points from the remaining leaves. Scoop out the choke (inner fibrous core).
2 Place artichokes into boiling, salted water with lemon juice.
3 Cook for about 20-30 minutes until tender, and drain.
4 Wash asparagus stalks gently, snap off woody end and scrape stalks to remove outer layer. Place asparagus into boiling, salted water. Cook for approximately 10 minutes, and drain.
5 Arrange the asparagus spears in the middle of a flat serving platter.
6 Slice the artichoke hearts thinly and arrange around asparagus.
7 Sprinkle with French Dressing and serve chilled.
Note: Canned artichoke hearts and asparagus spears can be substituted.

Zucchini Salad

Serves: 4   *150 kJ (35 cal) per serve*

1½ cups thinly sliced raw zucchini
3 spring onions or shallots, finely chopped

60 g (2 oz) mushrooms, peeled and sliced
2 medium tomatoes, cut into small wedges

Dressing
¼ cup tomato juice
1 tablespoon lemon juice
2 cloves garlic, crushed

pinch mixed dried herbs
salt and pepper

1 Place zucchini in a bowl with onions, mushrooms and tomatoes.
2 Mix dressing ingredients together. Pour over vegetables and marinate for 2 hours in the refrigerator before serving.

Tossed Salad

Serves: 4   *150 kJ (35 cal) per serve*

½ lettuce
2 medium tomatoes, cut in wedges
1 stalk celery, chopped
½ cucumber, sliced
½ green pepper (capsicum), sliced
2 tablespoons chopped fresh parsley

1 tablespoon chopped fresh chives
1 tablespoon chopped spring onions
1 clove garlic, crushed
salt and black pepper
1 quantity Italian Dressing (see page 59)

1 Wash lettuce and tear into bite-size pieces. Place in a salad bowl with other vegetables and seasonings.
2 Toss lightly in dressing. Serve immediately.

Marinated Mushrooms

Serves: 4   *100 kJ (25 cal) per serve*

250 g (8 oz) fresh mushrooms
1 clove garlic
1 teaspoon French mustard
½ teaspoon Worcestershire sauce

½ cup cider vinegar or lemon juice
salt
liquid artificial sweetener

Garnish
black pepper, freshly ground
1 teaspoon chopped fresh parsley
1 teaspoon chopped fresh chives

1 Slice mushrooms and place into a flat dish.
2 Chop garlic and add to mushrooms.
3 Add mustard, Worcestershire sauce, vinegar or lemon juice, salt and artificial sweetener to taste.
4 Marinate overnight in the refrigerator.
5 Serve chilled, sprinkled with black pepper, parsley and chives.

Sweet and Sour Red Cabbage (page 73)

Russian Salad

Serves: 4
Cooking time: 6 minutes

165 kJ (40 cal) per serve

125 g (4 oz) carrot, diced
120 g (4 oz) green peas
salt

2 tablespoons buttermilk
1 teaspoon finely chopped fresh mint
black pepper, freshly ground

1 Cook carrots for 3 minutes in salted water.
2 Add peas and boil for a further 3 minutes.
3 Drain and cool vegetables.
4 Stir in buttermilk, mint and black pepper.
5 Serve chilled.

Orange Fantasia

Serves: 4

410 kJ (90 cal) per serve

2 oranges
1 small onion, sliced
½ cucumber, sliced

½ quantity Creamy Orange Dressing (see
  page 60)

Garnish
parsley, chopped

1 Peel oranges, removing pith. Slice and arrange in alternating layers with onion and cucumber.
2 Pour dressing over salad and refrigerate at least 1 hour prior to serving.
3 Garnish with chopped parsley.

Asparagus Vinaigrette

Serves: 4

65 kJ (15 cal) per serve

500 g (1 lb) fresh asparagus or 1½ cups
  canned asparagus spears, drained
1 quantity Italian Dressing (see page 59)

1 If using fresh asparagus, wash stalks gently, snap off woody end and scrape stalks to remove the outer layer. Cook in boiling salted water until tender.
2 Drain and pour dressing over asparagus.
3 Cover and chill for 2 hours prior to serving.

Bean Salad

Serves: 4   *170 kJ (40 cal) per serve*

250 g (8 oz) whole green beans
1 red pepper (capsicum), finely chopped
½ onion, finely chopped

Marinade

¼ cup vinegar   **1 teaspoon polyunsaturated oil**
4 drops artificial liquid sweetener   **1 tablespoon chopped fresh chives**
½ teaspoon salt   **1 tablespoon chopped fresh parsley**
black pepper   **pinch mixed dried herbs**

1 Top and tail beans and remove any strings. Cook whole in salted water until tender. Drain and cool. Place in a serving dish.
2 Add red pepper (capsicum) and onion to beans.
3 Mix marinade ingredients together and pour over vegetables.
4 Chill thoroughly before serving.

Southern Beets

Serves: 4   *135 kJ (30 cal) per serve*

1 cup diced cooked beetroot   **6 drops artificial sweetener**
¼ cup chopped unsweetened pineapple **¼ cup unsweetened pineapple juice**
** pieces**   **salt and pepper**
¼ cup vinegar

1 Combine beetroot and pineapple in a bowl.
2 Add vinegar, sweetener, pineapple juice, salt and pepper. Marinate for at least 1 hour in the refrigerator prior to serving.

Yoghurt Crunch

Serves: 4   *170 kJ (40 cal) per serve*

1 cup diced apple   **4 tablespoons non-fat natural yoghurt**
1 cup grated carrot   **¼ teaspoon liquid artificial sweetener**
1 stalk celery, diced

1 Combine all ingredients.
2 Chill thoroughly before serving.

Asparagus and Zucchini Salad

Serves: 6   *140 kJ (35 cal) per serve*
Cooking time: 8 minutes

500 g (1 lb) fresh asparagus   **3 tablespoons non-fat natural yoghurt**
180 g (6 oz) zucchini   **paprika**
salt

1   Wash asparagus stalks gently, snap off woody end, and scrape white part with a knife to remove the outer layer. Cut into pieces 4 cm (1½ in) long.
2   Cut zucchini into similar sized pieces.
3   Place asparagus into boiling, salted water and simmer for 3 minutes.
4   Add zucchini and simmer for a further 5 minutes.
5   Drain and chill.
6   Gently stir in yoghurt, sprinkle with paprika. Serve.

Bean Shoot Salad

Serves: 4   *55 kJ (15 cal) per serve*
Cooking time: 2 minutes

1 cup fresh bean shoots   **¼ cup grated carrot**
salt   **2 tablespoons French Dressing (see**
¼ cup green pepper (capsicum)   **page 60)**
¼ cup celery

1   Drop bean shoots into boiling, salted water and simmer for 2 minutes. Drain and chill.
2   Cut pepper and celery into strips approximately the size of matchsticks.
3   Toss vegetables lightly with French dressing. Serve chilled.

Apricot Salad

Serves: 4   *490 kJ (115 cal) per serve*

250 g (8 oz) fresh apricots   **1 tablespoon chopped fresh mint**
1½ cups non-fat cottage cheese   **4 cup-shaped lettuce leaves**

Garnish
4 sprigs mint

1   Halve apricots, removing the stones. Reserve 8 halves and finely chop the remainder.
2   Combine cottage cheese, mint and chopped apricots.
3   Place lettuce leaves on serving dishes. Spoon cottage cheese mixture into the leaves. Place apricot halves over the cheese.
4   Garnish with a sprig of mint. Chill and serve.

Waldorf Salad

Serves: 6   *505 kJ (120 cal) per serve*

2 red apples
1 cup diced celery
1 tablespoon lemon juice

60 g (2 oz) walnuts, chopped
salt
¾ cup non-fat natural yoghurt

1 Wash and polish apples. Leaving skin on, remove core and dice neatly.
2 In serving bowl, combine apples, celery and lemon juice.
3 Blend walnuts and salt with yoghurt and lightly fold into apple and celery mixture.
4 Chill well before serving.

Cucumber Salad

Serves: 4   *125 kJ (30 cal) per serve*

1 medium cucumber, peeled
1 medium onion, sliced
salt
1 clove garlic, crushed

1 tablespoon wine vinegar
½ teaspoon dried dill
½ cup non-fat natural yoghurt
1 tablespoon finely chopped fresh mint

1 Slice cucumber finely. Place in serving dish with onion, salt, garlic, wine vinegar and dill.
2 Refrigerate for 30 minutes, drain off liquid.
3 Blend liquid with yoghurt until smooth.
4 Fold yoghurt dressing into cucumbers until well coated.
5 Chill before serving. Garnish with mint.

Copper Pennies

Serves: 4   *175 kJ (40 cal) per serve*
Cooking time: 5 minutes

125 g (4 oz) carrots, sliced thinly
4 mandarins
1 tablespoon chopped fresh mint

2 tablespoons orange juice
1 tablespoon lemon juice

1 Cook carrots in boiling, salted water for 5 minutes, drain and place in salad bowl.
2 Peel mandarins. Remove as much pith as possible, then cut into segments, discarding all membranes. Add to carrots.
3 Add mint, orange and lemon juice and toss well. Chill for at least 1 hour before serving.

Tomato Cups

Serves: 4   *195 kJ (45 cal) per serve*

4 medium tomatoes
½ cup finely chopped celery
¼ cup finely chopped onion
¼ cup chopped tinned asparagus tips
1 small green pepper (capsicum), finely
chopped

1 small red pepper (capsicum), finely
chopped
½ quantity Italian Dressing (see page 59)
4 cup-shaped lettuce leaves

Garnish
mint or parsley sprigs

1   Remove tops from tomatoes and reserve. Scoop out pulp. Discard seeds and dice flesh finely. Chill tomato cases.
2   Combine celery, onion, asparagus tips, peppers (capsicums) and diced tomato with dressing.
3   Marinate vegetables in the refrigerator for 1 hour.
4   Fill tomato cases with the mixture. Replace tomato tops.
5   Serve on lettuce leaves, garnished with a sprig of mint or parsley.

Tomato and Onion Salad

Serves: 4   *90 kJ (20 cal) per serve*

250 g (8 oz) tomatoes, sliced
1 medium onion, sliced

Dressing
½ cup brown vinegar
4-6 drops artificial sweetener
salt and pepper

Garnish
chopped parsley

1   Layer tomato and onion in dish.
2   Combine vinegar, sweetener, salt and pepper, and pour over vegetables.
3   Marinate for at least 1 hour in the refrigerator prior to serving. Sprinkle with parsley.

SALAD DRESSINGS

Yoghurt Dressing

Yield: ¾ cup   *295 kJ (70 cal) per recipe*

½ cup non-fat natural yoghurt
½ teaspoon dry mustard
2 tablespoons vinegar

3 drops liquid artificial sweetener
garlic salt
black pepper

1   Stir yoghurt to remove any lumps.
2   Add mustard, vinegar and sweetener.
3   Add garlic salt and pepper to taste.
4   Cover and store in refrigerator until required.

Buttermilk Dressing

Yield: 1½ cups   *570 kJ (135 cal) per recipe*

¾ cup buttermilk
½ small onion, finely diced
¼ cup finely chopped celery
1 medium red pepper (capsicum), finely
   chopped

2 tablespoons chopped fresh parsley
rind of 1 lemon, grated
juice of 1 lemon
salt and pepper
1 clove garlic, crushed

1   Combine all ingredients, cover and refrigerate until required.

Italian Dressing

Yield: ¾ cup   *35 kJ (10 cal) per recipe*

½ cup vinegar
1 tablespoon lemon juice
2 tablespoons chopped fresh parsley
1 tablespoon chopped fresh chives
1 clove of garlic, crushed

½ teaspoon dry mustard
garlic salt
black pepper
3 drops liquid artificial sweetener

1   Combine above ingredients.
2   Cover, shake well, and refrigerate.

Horseradish–Cucumber Dressing

Yield: 1½ cups   *690 kJ (165 cal) per recipe*

½ cup peeled and grated cucumber
1 cup non-fat natural yoghurt
pinch garlic salt
2 teaspoons prepared horseradish sauce

2 teaspoons finely sliced spring onion or
   shallots
1 tablespoon finely chopped fresh mint

1   Combine cucumber in bowl with yoghurt, garlic salt, horseradish, spring onion
    and mint. Mix well.
2   Chill until ready to serve.

Creamy Orange Dressing

Yield: 1½ cups   *140 kJ (35 cal) per recipe*

1 cup non-fat natural yoghurt
6 tablespoons unsweetened orange juice
   concentrate

2 tablespoons finely chopped fresh parsley
2 spring onions, finely chopped

1   Combine all ingredients and chill.

Curry Dressing

Yield: ½ cup   *305 kJ (75 cal) per recipe*

½ cup non-fat natural yoghurt
½ teaspoon curry powder
pinch garlic salt

pinch paprika
2 tablespoons chopped fresh parsley

1   Mix yoghurt with all other ingredients.
2   Check flavour and chill until ready to use.

Herbed Tomato Dressing

Yield: 1 cup   *420 kJ (100 cal) per recipe*

½ cup unsweetened tomato juice
4 tablespoons tomato paste
1 clove garlic, crushed
1 tablespoon chopped fresh parsley
1 tablespoon chopped fresh chives

salt
black pepper
few drops Tabasco sauce
pinch of thyme, basil, and marjoram
2 tablespoons non-fat natural yoghurt

1   Combine tomato juice and tomato paste in a bowl.
2   Add garlic, parsley, chives, salt, pepper, Tabasco sauce, and herbs. Mix well.
3   Add yoghurt and stir until well blended.
4   Refrigerate until ready to use.

French Dressing

Yield: ½ cup   *55 kJ (15 cal) per recipe*

1 teaspoon gelatine
¼ cup cold water
3 tablespoons lemon juice
salt and pepper

pinch dry mustard
1 clove garlic, crushed
1 teaspoon finely chopped white onion
2 drops liquid artificial sweetener

1   Soften gelatine in cold water, and dissolve over hot water; cool.
2   Combine the lemon juice, salt, pepper, mustard, garlic, onion, and sweetener.
3   Add to the gelatine and shake well.
4   Cover and store in the refrigerator.
5   Remove from the refrigerator and leave at room temperature for at least 1
    hour before serving. Shake well again before serving.

Tartare Sauce

Yield: 1 cup   *610 kJ (145 cal) per recipe*

1 cup non-fat natural yoghurt
1 dill cucumber, chopped
2 teaspoons chopped capers
2 teaspoons finely chopped mixed fresh herbs (use at least 3 of the following —

chervil, chives, tarragon, fennel, basil, rosemary, thyme), or ¼ teaspoon dried mixed herbs
3 teaspoons finely chopped fresh parsley

1 Blend all ingredients together.
2 Cover and store in the refrigerator.

Cocktail Sauce

Yield: ½ cup   *240 kJ (55 cal) per recipe*

4 tablespoons non-fat natural yoghurt
4 teaspoons tomato paste
4 drops liquid artificial sweetener
salt and pepper

pinch garlic salt
2 teaspoons finely chopped fresh parsley
pinch dry mustard

1 Mix all ingredients together.
2 Cover and store in the refrigerator.

VEGETABLES

Vegetables are often the neglected part of many meals. As most vegetables are virtually fat and cholesterol free, and yet good sources of vitamins and minerals, we feel their significance should not be overlooked in the planning of any diet.

Have you ever thought of serving a main course consisting of four or five well-prepared vegetables of the season, accompanied by a tangy sauce? We hope that the recipes in this section may add new life to the vegetables you serve at mealtimes.

Try to remember the following hints when next preparing vegetables:

- Peel vegetables only when absolutely necessary. Peelings contain important fibre and often the valuable vitamins and minerals. Potatoes, carrots and pumpkin can all be served with the skin intact—simply scrub well before cooking to remove surface soil.
- Cook vegetables whole or in large pieces. Vitamin losses (particularly vitamins B and C) are rapid when vegetables are diced or cut into small slices. If smaller pieces are desired, cook quickly in a minimum of liquid so nutrients are retained.
- To give vegetables a lift, why not add a clove of garlic, finely diced onions, fresh herbs or grated nutmeg? Alternative cooking liquids can be tomato or lemon juice, chicken stock or wine.
- Avoid the use of sodium bicarbonate when cooking green vegetables. The soda destroys the vitamins present in the food and imparts an unpleasant flavour and taste to the vegetables.
- For the best results when cooking green vegetables, plunge the vegetables quickly into boiling water, cook rapidly, and drain while still firm.
- Fresh vegetables keep their colour and texture best when they are cooked until just tender. Steaming is an ideal way to retain colour, shape, nutrients and flavour.

Chinese Steamed Vegetables (page 75)

Beans Vinaigrette

Serves: 4   170 kJ (40 cal) per serve
Cooking time: 10 minutes

250 g (8 oz) fresh green beans
salt
¼ teaspoon dry mustard
1 tablespoon white vinegar

2 teaspoons chopped fresh parsley
2 teaspoons chopped fresh chives
pepper
2 teaspoons polyunsaturated oil

1 Top and tail beans, boil in salted water until tender; drain.
2 Combine salt, mustard, vinegar, parsley, chives and pepper in a small bowl.
   Mix with oil.
3 Pour sauce over beans.
4 Beans may be served hot or chilled.

Beans Parisienne

Serves: 4   310 kJ (75 cal) per serve
Cooking time: 15 minutes

250 g (8 oz) fresh green beans
1 teaspoon polyunsaturated margarine
30 g (1 oz) blanched almonds, slivered

1 teaspoon lemon juice
garlic salt
black pepper

1 Top and tail beans, boil in salted water until tender; drain.
2 Melt margarine in a frying pan, add almonds and cook until lightly browned.
3 Combine beans, almonds, lemon juice, garlic salt and pepper. Serve hot.

Beans and Zucchini

Serves: 4   105 kJ (25 cal) per serve
Cooking time: 8 minutes

250 g (8 oz) fresh green beans
1 medium zucchini
salt

1 String beans and cut into pieces 10 cm (4 in) long.
2 Cut zucchini into strips of similar size to beans.
3 Cook beans in boiling salted water for 5 minutes.
4 Add zucchini and cook for a further 3 minutes, drain and serve.

Broccoli in Tomato Juice

Serves: 4   100 kJ (25 cal) per serve
Cooking time: 5 minutes

250 g (8 oz) fresh broccoli
2 cups water

salt
4 tablespoons tomato juice

1 Cut broccoli into flowerettes. If stems are thick, slice ½ inch into base to help
   cook more quickly.
2 Add broccoli to boiling salted water and cook rapidly for 4 minutes. Drain.
3 Add tomato juice, cook for a further minute, stirring gently. Serve.

Lemon Broccoli

Serves: 4
Cooking time: 30 minutes
Oven temperature: 180°C (350°F)

140 kJ (35 cal) per serve

1 bunch fresh broccoli
1 lemon, sliced
garlic salt

black pepper
1 tablespoon water

1 Trim leaves and tough stalks from broccoli. Place in an ovenproof casserole and cover with lemon slices.
2 Sprinkle with garlic salt and pepper, add water.
3 Cover with aluminium foil and bake for 30 minutes at 180°C (350°F). Serve.

Aubergine Bake

Serves: 4
Cooking time: 30 minutes
Oven temperature: 190°C (375°F)

180 kJ (45 cal) per serve

250 g (8 oz) aubergine (eggplant), cut into
  thick slices
2 medium tomatoes, sliced
1 medium apple, sliced

salt
black pepper, freshly ground
2 tablespoons water

1 Place vegetables and apple in layers in a small casserole or baking dish. Sprinkle between layers with salt and pepper.
2 Finish with a layer of tomato.
3 Pour over water and bake in the oven at 190°C (375°F) for 30 minutes.

Ratatouille

Serves: 8
Cooking time: 1 hour
Oven temperature: 180°C (350°F)

310 kJ (75 cal) per serve

250 g (8 oz) aubergine (eggplant), diced
salt
1 tablespoon polyunsaturated oil
1 large onion, chopped
3 cloves garlic, crushed
3 zucchini, sliced
3 tomatoes, roughly chopped
2 stalks celery, cut into 2.5 cm (1 in) pieces

2 green peppers (capsicums), roughly
  chopped
1 chicken stock cube
garlic salt
pepper
pinch dried basil
pinch dried thyme
2 starch-reduced biscuits, crushed

Garnish
parsley, chopped

1 Sprinkle aubergine with salt and set aside for 30 minutes to draw out juices. Pat dry with a paper towel.
2 Heat oil, cook onion and garlic until soft.
3 Combine all ingredients together in a casserole, sprinkle with crushed biscuits.
4 Cover tightly and cook in the oven at 180°C (350°F) for 45 minutes.
5 Uncover and place under a hot griller until brown. Serve, sprinkled with parsley.

Herbed Chokos

Serves: 4
Cooking time: 30 minutes
Oven temperature: 180°C (350°F)

115 kJ (30 cal) per serve

2 chokos
2 medium tomatoes, sliced
salt

black pepper, freshly ground
½ teaspoon mixed dried herbs
2 tablespoons water

1 Peel, quarter, stone and slice chokos.
2 Place chokos and tomatoes in layers in a small casserole dish. Sprinkle between layers with salt, pepper and herbs.
3 Add water, cover and bake in the oven at 180°C (350°F) for 30 minutes.

Curried Brussels Sprouts

Serves: 4
Cooking time: 10 minutes

275 kJ (65 cal) per serve

500 g (1 lb) Brussels sprouts, trimmed and slit through base
1 teaspoon polyunsaturated margarine
4 spring onions or shallots, finely sliced

1 stalk celery, finely chopped
1 level teaspoon curry powder
garlic salt

1 Cook sprouts for 5 minutes in boiling, salted water; drain.
2 Melt margarine in a frying pan or saucepan. Add spring onions or shallots and celery, toss until lightly cooked.
3 Add curry powder and garlic salt and cook for 2-3 minutes.
4 Add sprouts and toss until all ingredients are well mixed. Serve.

Aubergine Neapolitan

Serves: 6
Cooking time: 1 hour 15 minutes
Oven temperature: 190°C (375°F)

275 kJ (65 cal) per serve

500 g (1 lb) aubergine (eggplant)
salt
2 teaspoons polyunsaturated oil
500 g (1 lb) tomatoes, sliced

2 medium onions, sliced
salt and pepper
pinch mixed dried herbs
1 clove garlic, crushed

1 Cut aubergine into 5 mm (¼ in) slices. Place on a flat tray, sprinkle with salt and leave for 1 hour to draw out the juices. Pat dry with a paper towel.
2 Heat oil in a frying pan. Fry aubergine slices until brown.
3 Place vegetables in layers in an ovenproof casserole. Sprinkle each layer with salt and pepper.
4 Sprinkle top layer with salt, pepper and herbs. Add crushed garlic.
5 Bake in the oven at 190°C (375°F) for 1 hour.

Foreground: *Herbed Chokos;* background: *Curried Brussels Sprouts*

Mushrooms à La Grecque

Serves: 4
Cooking time: 1 hour

275 kJ (65 cal) per serve

2 cups Chicken Stock (see page 45)
½ cup dry white wine
1 tablespoon polyunsaturated oil
3 tablespoons lemon juice
2 large garlic cloves, sliced

½ teaspoon dried thyme
6 peppercorns
salt
375 g (12 oz) fresh mushrooms, peeled and
  stalks removed

Garnish
parsley, chopped
4 lemon slices

1 Place all ingredients except mushrooms in a large saucepan.
2 Bring to the boil, partially cover saucepan and simmer slowly for 45 minutes.
3 Using a fine sieve, strain marinade into a bowl.
4 Return marinade to the saucepan. Bring to the boil.
5 Drop in mushrooms, cover and simmer for 10 minutes.
6 Transfer mushrooms and marinade to a shallow dish.
7 Chill thoroughly before serving.
8 Garnish with parsley and lemon slices.

Tomato and Onion Pie

Serves: 4
Cooking time: 30 minutes
Oven temperature: 190°C (375°F)

100 kJ (25 cal) per serve

2 large tomatoes, sliced
1 large white onion, sliced
pinch mixed dried herbs

salt
black pepper, freshly ground
2 tablespoons water

1 Place vegetables in layers in a small casserole or baking dish, sprinkling between layers with herbs, salt and pepper.
2 Finish with a layer of tomato.
3 Pour water over vegetables and bake in the oven at 190°C (375°F) for 30 minutes.

Mushrooms Paprika

Serves: 4
Cooking time: 15 minutes

265 kJ (60 cal) per serve

2 teaspoons polyunsaturated margarine
1 medium onion, finely chopped
500 g (1 lb) fresh mushrooms, peeled and
  stalks removed

½ teaspoon paprika
salt and pepper

Garnish
2 tablespoons non-fat natural yoghurt
sprinkle paprika

1 Melt margarine in a frying pan, add onion and fry until soft.
2 Chop mushrooms and add to pan. Cook until soft.
3 Add paprika, salt and pepper, stir in well. Check flavour.
4 Serve hot, topped with yoghurt and sprinkled with paprika.

Tomatoes Stuffed with Asparagus

Serves: 4
Cooking time: 10 minutes

250 kJ (60 cal) per serve

4 medium tomatoes
garlic salt
pepper

1½ cups drained, canned asparagus cuts
4 spring onions or shallots, sliced finely
2 teaspoons polyunsaturated margarine

1 Slice tops off tomatoes and scoop out pulp, leaving skins intact. Discard pulp.
2 Sprinkle garlic salt and pepper over inside of cases and fill with asparagus.
3 Sprinkle with spring onions, and top with ½ teaspoon polyunsaturated margarine.
4 Place under a hot griller until tomatoes are tender and top lightly browned. Serve.

Asparagus with Mushrooms

Serves: 6
Cooking time: 15 minutes

115 kJ (25 cal) per serve

1½ cups asparagus spears (fresh or canned)
2 teaspoons polyunsaturated margarine
125 g (4 oz) fresh mushrooms

garlic salt
black pepper
2 tablespoons dry white wine

Garnish
parsley, chopped

1 Cook fresh asparagus or heat canned asparagus.
2 Heat margarine in a frying pan, add mushrooms and fry until tender.
3 Add remaining ingredients and cook until wine has almost evaporated.
4 Place drained asparagus in a serving dish.
5 Spoon mushrooms over asparagus leaving tips exposed. Sprinkle with chopped parsley.

Pumpkin and Mushrooms

Serves: 4
Cooking time: 20 minutes

205 kJ (50 cal) per serve

500 g (1 lb) pumpkin
125 g (4 oz) fresh mushrooms, sliced
salt and pepper

1 clove garlic
1 cup unsweetened tomato juice

1 Peel pumpkin and slice into pieces about 1 cm (½ in) thick.
2 Place pumpkin and mushrooms into a saucepan and sprinkle with salt and pepper.
3 Crush garlic over vegetables.
4 Pour over tomato juice, cover and cook until vegetables are tender (approximately 20 minutes).

Vegetables en Brochette

Serves: 4
Cooking time: 15 minutes

210 kJ (50 cal) per serve

180 g (6 oz) tomatoes
180 g (6 oz) white onions
180 g (6 oz) green peppers (capsicums)

120 g (4 oz) button mushrooms
12 x 18 cm (7 in) skewers

Sauce
1 tablespoon soy sauce
2 tablespoons lemon juice
3-4 drops artificial liquid sweetener

1 Wash all vegetables.
2 Cut tomatoes and onions into 2 cm (¾ in) cubes, green peppers into 2 cm (¾ in) squares and trim stems from mushrooms.
3 Thread pieces of tomato, onion, pepper and mushroom along skewers, leaving 2.5 cm (1 in) of skewer free at both ends.
4 Mix sauce and brush liberally over vegetables.
5 Grill until all vegetables are tender (approximately 7 minutes on either side), brushing with sauce at intervals to prevent drying.
6 Serve three hot skewers to each guest.

Zucchini in Tomato Juice

Serves: 4
Cooking time: 3 minutes

60 kJ (15 cal) per serve

1½ cups zucchini, sliced
½ cup water

salt
3 tablespoons unsweetened tomato juice

1 Simmer zucchini for 2 minutes in boiling, salted water; drain.
2 Add tomato juice and simmer for a further minute, stirring gently. Serve.

Zucchini with Yoghurt

Serves: 4
Cooking time: 3 minutes

65 kJ (15 cal) per serve

1½ cups zucchini, sliced
½ cup water

salt
1 tablespoon non-fat natural yoghurt

1 Simmer zucchini in boiling, salted water for 3 minutes; drain.
2 Gently stir in yoghurt and serve.

Silverbeet and Nutmeg

Serves: 4
Cooking time: 8 minutes

110 kJ (25 cal) per serve

1 bunch silverbeet or spinach
1 cup water

salt
¼ teaspoon ground nutmeg

1 Wash silverbeet well, remove and discard stalks.
2 Bring water to the boil with salt and nutmeg.
3 Add silverbeet and simmer covered for 8 minutes.
4 Drain well, chop through with a sharp knife and serve.

70

Silverbeet Oriental

Serves: 4
Cooking time: 10 minutes

225 kJ (55 cal) per serve

1 bunch silverbeet or spinach
2 tablespoons soy sauce
1 chicken stock cube
1 tablespoon dry sherry

black pepper
5 drops artificial liquid sweetener
2 teaspoons polyunsaturated margarine

1   Wash silverbeet well, remove and discard stalks. Chop leaves roughly.
2   Mix soy sauce, stock cube, sherry, pepper and artificial sweetener.
3   Heat margarine in a large frying pan, add silverbeet and braise for approximately 5 minutes. Add seasonings.
4   Cook for a further 5 minutes until silverbeet is tender.
5   Spoon liquid over silverbeet and serve.

Savoury Spinach

Serves: 4
Cooking time: 10 minutes

110 kJ (35 cal) per serve

1 bunch spinach or silverbeet
½ cup canned champignons, drained and sliced

pinch ground nutmeg
garlic salt
black pepper

1   Wash spinach carefully, remove coarse stalks.
2   Place all ingredients in a saucepan, cover and allow to steam, shaking occasionally, until spinach has wilted. Serve.

Stuffed Cabbage Leaves

Serves: 4
Cooking time: 1 hour
Oven temperature: 180°C (350°F)

345 kJ (80 cal) per serve

8 cabbage leaves
250 g (8 oz) pumpkin, finely chopped
2 medium onions, finely chopped
¼ cup finely chopped green pepper (capsicum)

½ cup finely chopped celery
1 chicken stock cube, crumbled
pinch mixed dried herbs
salt and pepper
2 cups tomato purée

1   Blanch cabbage leaves in boiling water until wilted. Remove the centre stalk.
2   Mix together pumpkin, onions, green pepper, celery, stock cube and seasonings.
3   Fold mixture into leaves and pack tightly into an ovenproof casserole. Cover with tomato purée.
4   Cover, and place in the oven for 1 hour at 180°C (350°F).
5   Spoon sauce over leaves and serve.

Sweet and Sour Red Cabbage

Serves: 6
Cooking time: 15 minutes

230 kJ (55 cal) per serve

½ small red cabbage
2 teaspoons polyunsaturated oil
1 green apple, finely diced
1 medium onion, finely chopped
½ cup unsweetened canned pineapple

pieces, drained and juice reserved
2 tablespoons unsweetened pineapple
juice from can
3 tablespoons white vinegar
salt and pepper

1 Remove centre stalk from cabbage, and slice cabbage finely.
2 Heat oil in a frying pan. Add cabbage, apple and onion and cook over a low heat for 5 minutes.
3 Add pineapple pieces, pineapple juice, vinegar, salt and pepper, cover and simmer for a further 10 minutes.
4 Serve hot.

Braised Cabbage

Serves: 4
Cooking time: 5 minutes

185 kJ (45 cal) per serve

2 teaspoons polyunsaturated oil
1 small white onion, diced
250 g (8 oz) cabbage, sliced

2 teaspoons water
2 teaspoons soy sauce
salt

1 Heat oil in a frying pan or saucepan, add onion, cabbage and water.
2 Toss well until vegetables are finely coated with oil and water.
3 Cover and cook gently for 4 minutes, tossing occasionally to prevent burning.
4 Add soy sauce and salt and toss for a further minute.
5 Serve hot.

Cabbage Medley

Serves: 6
Cooking time: 15 minutes

245 kJ (60 cal) per serve

2 teaspoons polyunsaturated margarine
1 chicken stock cube, crumbled
1 level teaspoon curry powder
1 large onion, finely chopped

250 g (8 oz) frozen green beans
juice of 1 lemon
3 cups shredded cabbage

Garnish
parsley, chopped

1 Melt margarine in a large frying pan. Add crumbled stock cube, curry powder and onion. Fry until onion is soft, but not browned.
2 Add beans and cook for 5 minutes.
3 Add lemon juice and cabbage. Cook mixture over a moderate heat for 10 minutes, stirring frequently.
4 Serve, garnished with parsley.

Italian Cabbage

Serves: 4
Cooking time: 20 minutes

155 kJ (35 cal) per serve

½ cabbage, cut into 4 wedges
1 cup unsweetened tomato juice
¼ teaspoon mixed dried herbs

salt and pepper
1 clove garlic, crushed

1 Pack cabbage wedges tightly into a saucepan.
2 Pour tomato juice over cabbage. Sprinkle with herbs, salt, pepper and garlic.
3 Cover saucepan and simmer gently until the cabbage is tender.
4 Spoon a little sauce over the wedges and serve.

Stuffed Aubergine

Serves: 4
Cooking time: 35-40 minutes
Oven temperature: 190°C (375°F)

215 kJ (50 cal) per serve

2 medium aubergines (eggplant)
1 large tomato, diced
1 medium onion, diced

100 g (3 oz) fresh mushrooms, diced
salt and pepper
¼ cup water

1 Slice aubergines in half, lengthwise. Scoop the flesh from centre of aubergine leaving about 1 cm (½ in) of flesh attached to skin. Dice flesh.
2 Place diced vegetables in a saucepan with salt, pepper and water.
3 Cook until tender, approximately 5 minutes.
4 Fill the aubergine cases with this mixture and bake in the oven at 190°C (375°F) for 30 minutes or until aubergine cases are soft to touch.

Savoury Tomatoes

Serves: 4
Cooking time: 15 minutes

250 kJ (60 cal) per serve

1 teaspoon polyunsaturated margarine
2 large onions, roughly chopped
500 g (1 lb) tomatoes, roughly chopped
2 cloves garlic, crushed

½ teaspoon mixed dried herbs
salt and pepper
1 tablespoon vinegar

Garnish
parsley or chives, chopped

1 Heat polyunsaturated margarine in frying pan.
2 Fry onions until soft, add tomatoes, garlic, herbs, salt, pepper and vinegar.
3 Cook over a high heat until the vegetable mixture thickens (texture should be fairly firm).
4 Garnish and serve.

Snow Peas

Serves: 4   45 kJ (10 cal) per serve
Cooking time: 3 minutes

1½ cups fresh snow peas
½ cup water
salt

1 Wash peas and remove stalks, leaving pod whole.
2 Simmer in salted water for 3 minutes, drain and serve.

Braised Onions

Serves: 4   175 kJ (40 cal) per serve
Cooking time: 20 minutes

1 cup cold water
1 chicken stock cube
500 g (1 lb) small onions, peeled

2 teaspoons polyunsaturated margarine
2 tablespoons dry white wine

Garnish
chives or parsley, chopped

1 Place water and stock cube in a saucepan. Bring to the boil.
2 Add onions, reduce heat and simmer until just tender (about 10 minutes).
3 Melt margarine in a frying pan.
4 Lift onions out of stock and place in the frying pan. Brown lightly. Add wine and allow to evaporate.
5 While onions are browning, reduce stock over a high heat to 2 tablespoons.
6 Add stock to onions in the pan.
7 Serve sprinkled with chives or parsley.

Chinese Steamed Vegetables

Serves: 6   300 kJ (70 cal) per serve
Cooking time: 10-12 minutes

½ Chinese cabbage
1 tablespoon polyunsaturated oil
1 medium white onion, quartered
185 g (6 oz) broccoli, cut into flowerettes
1 medium carrot, sliced

1 cup snow peas (optional)
1 cup bean shoots
125 g (4 oz) mushrooms, sliced
1 chicken stock cube
salt

1 Chop Chinese cabbage into pieces, approximately 5 cm (2 in) long, keeping stalks and leaves separate.
2 Heat oil in a wok or large frying pan, add onion, cook for 1 minute.
3 Add stalks of cabbage, broccoli, carrots and snow peas and fry for 2 minutes longer, stirring continuously.
4 Add cabbage leaves, bean shoots, mushrooms, stock cube and salt, stir, cover and cook for 3 minutes. Serve.

Braised Bean Shoots

Serves: 4
Cooking time: 3 minutes

55 kJ (15 cal) per serve

2 cups bean shoots, washed
½ cup thinly sliced celery
½ cup water

salt
1 teaspoon soy sauce

1 Simmer vegetables in boiling, salted water for 3 minutes.
2 Drain vegetables, add soy sauce and serve.

Mashed Carrot and Parsnip

Serves: 4
Cooking time: 15 minutes

195 kJ (45 cal) per serve

2 medium carrots
1 medium parsnip

salt
1 tablespoon liquid skim milk

Garnish
4 sprigs parsley

1 Peel carrots and parsnip and chop roughly into small pieces.
2 Place into boiling, salted water and simmer for 15 minutes or until tender.
3 Drain, add skim milk and mash vegetables together.
4 Serve garnished with parsley.

Orange-Glazed Parsnips

Serves: 4
Cooking time: 20 minutes

330 kJ (80 cal) per serve

250 g (8 oz) parsnips, peeled and sliced
½ cup orange juice

1 teaspoon grated orange rind
2 teaspoons polyunsaturated margarine

1 Cook parsnips in boiling, salted water until tender (about 5-10 minutes).
2 Drain off water, add orange juice, orange rind and polyunsaturated margarine, and cook a further 10 minutes.
3 Lift parsnips out of the saucepan, place in a serving dish and keep hot.
4 Boil liquid in the saucepan until it has thickened. Pour over parsnips and serve.

Witloof and Tomato

Serves: 4
Cooking time: 5 minutes

60 kJ (15 cal) per serve

1 medium witloof
2 medium tomatoes
1 clove garlic

salt
2 teaspoons water

1 Trim witloof, cut in half, break into leaves, wash and drain.
2 Cut tomato into wedges.
3 Crush garlic and place into a saucepan.
4 Add witloof, tomato, salt and water.
5 Cover and cook for 5 minutes, tossing occasionally.

Devilled Carrots

Serves: 4
Cooking time: 15 minutes   *145 kJ (35 cal) per serve*

375 g (12 oz) carrots, peeled and diced
salt
½ teaspoon prepared mustard
5 drops Tabasco sauce

5 drops Worcestershire sauce
salt and pepper
pinch paprika

Garnish
2 teaspoons chopped parsley or chives

1   Place carrots in boiling, salted water and cook for 10 minutes. Drain.
2   Add mustard, Tabasco, Worcestershire sauce, salt, pepper and paprika. Reheat, tossing frequently.
3   Garnish with parsley or chives.

Braised Carrots

Serves: 4
Cooking time: 20 minutes   *220 kJ (55 cal) per serve*

2 chicken stock cubes
1½ cups water
375 g (12 oz) carrots, peeled and sliced

1 medium onion, finely chopped
1 teaspoon polyunsaturated margarine

Garnish
parsley, chopped

1   Add chicken stock cubes to water and bring to the boil. Add carrots and onion.
2   Cook uncovered until carrots are tender, drain liquid.
3   Add margarine and parsley. Toss and serve.

Leek and Apple

Serves: 4
Cooking time: 8 minutes   *150 kJ (35 cal) per serve*

1 leek
1 teaspoon polyunsaturated oil

1 cooking apple, sliced
salt

1   Slice leek, discarding the roots and coarse leaves, wash well.
2   Heat oil in a saucepan.
3   Toss leeks and apples in the pan.
4   Add salt, cover the pan and cook for 8 minutes.

FISH

Those who can purchase fish readily and cheaply are indeed lucky. Fish is a good source of protein, low in fat and yet moderate in kilojoule (calorie) content. Whether you use fresh or canned fish, we suggest that it becomes a regular feature on the menu at home.

Here are some helpful hints for preparing and cooking fish:

- When selecting fresh fish look for these characteristics: eyes bright and full, gills bright red, flesh firm to the touch and no fishy odour.
- When buying canned salmon or tuna select products that are prepared in brine (salt water).
- Thaw frozen fish in the refrigerator to minimise bacterial contamination. Never refreeze thawed fish.
- Fish that is properly cooked will flake with a fork.
- To prevent fish from drying out when baking or grilling, spoon the fish regularly with a marinade made from any of the following ingredients: soy sauce, lemon juice, wine, fish stock, tomato juice or orange juice.
- A serving of 185 g (6 oz) of fish per person has been allowed in the recipes in this section.
- Shellfish (prawns, scallops, oysters, crayfish) are high in cholesterol, so we have not used them in our recipes. We suggest that these seafoods be served only on special occasions and taken in moderation.

Foil-Wrapped Trout (page 81)

Paprika Fish

Serves: 4
Cooking time: 25 minutes

735 kJ (185 cal) per serve

1 onion, sliced
2 teaspoons polyunsaturated margarine
2 teaspoons paprika
4 fillets bream or perch, weighing about 750 g (1½ lb) in total
¼ cup dry white wine

1 tablespoon tomato paste
½ teaspoon salt
pinch black pepper
juice of ½ lemon
2 tablespoons non-fat natural yoghurt

Garnish
lemon wedges
parsley, chopped

1   Fry onion lightly in margarine. Add paprika and cook for a further 4 minutes.
2   Add fish and wine and cook until fish is cooked through.
3   Lift fish onto a heated serving platter and keep warm.
4   Add tomato paste to pan. Stir in well. Add salt, pepper and lemon juice. Mix well together.
5   Remove pan from heat. Stir in yoghurt, and pour sauce over fish.
6   Garnish with lemon wedges and parsley.

Fish Roll

Serves: 4
Cooking time: 10 minutes
Oven temperature: 180°C (350°F)

755 kJ (180 cal) per serve

90 g (3 oz) zucchini
90 g (3 oz) fresh asparagus spears
salt
4 fillets white fish, weighing about 750 g (1½ lb) in total

1 tablespoon lemon juice
1 cup liquid skim milk

1   Cut zucchini into pieces 4 cm (1½ in) long.
2   Wash asparagus, snap off woody end, and scrape white part of stalk with a knife to remove outer layer.
3   Simmer asparagus and zucchini in boiling, salted water for 5 minutes. Drain.
4   Wash fish fillets and rub with lemon juice.
5   Divide asparagus and zucchini into 4 and place one portion on each fillet of fish.
6   Roll up and secure with wooden toothpicks.
7   Place in a flat baking dish and sprinkle with salt.
8   Pour over skim milk, cover and bake in the oven at 180°C (350°F) for 10 minutes.
9   Remove toothpicks and serve.

Foil-Wrapped Trout

Serves: 4
Cooking time: 10 minutes

1525 kJ (380 cal) per serve

4 whole rainbow trout
salt, for cleaning
2 tablespoons chopped spring onions
   or shallots
½ cup peeled and chopped fresh
   mushrooms

2 tablespoons finely chopped fresh parsley
1 tablespoon dry white wine
salt and pepper
4 slices lemon
4 tablespoons lemon juice

1   Gut and scale fish. Remove heads. Rinse fish. Sprinkle inside with salt.
2   Mix onions, mushrooms, parsley, wine, salt and pepper.
3   Fill fish with mixture.
4   Place each fish on a piece of aluminium foil.
5   Brush with lemon juice, sprinkle with salt and pepper. Place a slice of lemon on
    each fish, wrap in foil and seal edges carefully.
6   Place under a hot griller. Turn once during cooking to ensure even cooking, or
    bake in oven at 180°C (350°F) for 30 minutes.

Whiting à l'Orange

Serves: 4
Cooking time: 20 minutes

895 kJ (215 cal) per serve

1 tablespoon polyunsaturated margarine
4 whiting fillets, skinned, weighing about
   750 g (1½ lb) in total

2 tablespoons finely chopped onion
¼ cup dry white wine
1 cup orange juice

1   Heat margarine in a frying pan. Add fish. Cook on both sides until golden.
2   Remove fish and keep hot on a covered plate.
3   Pour off any margarine remaining in the pan. Add all the other ingredients and
    simmer until the mixture has reduced to a thick sauce.
4   Strain sauce over fish and serve.

Mediterranean Fish Bake

Serves: 4
Cooking time: 15 minutes
Oven temperature: 180°C (350°F)

4 fillets white fish, cut thickly, weighing
   about 750 g (1½ lb) in total
1 tablespoon lemon juice
1 medium tomato
60 g (2 oz) mushrooms

690 kJ (165 cal) per serve

½ medium onion
½ medium green pepper (capsicum)
salt and pepper
½ teaspoon dried oregano
½ cup water

1   Wash fish, rub with lemon juice and place in a flat baking dish.
2   Dice tomato, mushrooms, onion and green pepper and sprinkle over fish.
3   Sprinkle with salt, pepper and herbs.
4   Pour water into the dish, cover and bake in the oven at 180°C (350°F) for 15
    minutes.

Whole Fish in Black Bean Sauce

Serves: 4
Cooking time: 20-30 minutes
Oven temperature: 180°C (350°F)

960 kJ (240 cal) per serve

4 whole bream or small schnapper
juice of 2 lemons
1 cup water
salt
2 tablespoons black beans
2 teaspoons brandy
1 tablespoon soy sauce
½ clove garlic, crushed

½ teaspoon finely chopped green ginger
½ teaspoon monosodium glutamate
2 teaspoons polyunsaturated oil
½ cup diced green pepper (capsicum)
½ cup diced red pepper (capsicum), or
**   par-boiled carrot rings**
1 medium white onion, quartered
salt

1 Gut, scale and wash fish. Remove heads and discard.
2 Place into a flat casserole dish.
3 Pour over lemon juice, ½ cup water and sprinkle with salt.
4 Cover dish and bake in an oven at 180°C (350°F) for 20-30 minutes, depending on the size of the fish.
5 Pour sufficient boiling water over black beans to cover, stand for 10 minutes and drain.
6 Mash black beans, using a fork, with brandy, soy sauce, garlic, green ginger and monosodium glutamate.
7 Heat oil in a wok or frying pan.
8 Add peppers, onion and salt. Fry for 3 minutes, stirring continuously. Remove from pan.
9 Place the black bean mixture into the pan and cook for 1 minute.
10 Return the peppers and onion to the pan, add ½ cup water, and simmer for a further minute.
11 Drain liquid from fish in casserole dish and discard. Pour sauce over the fish.
12 Return to the oven for 2 minutes to combine flavours. Serve immediately.

Baked Fish Albert

Serves: 4
Cooking time: 20 minutes
Oven temperature: 180°C (350°F)

705 kJ (170 cal) per serve

4 whole white fish
2 medium onions
2 cloves garlic
1 tablespoon finely chopped fresh parsley
1 tablespoon finely chopped fresh chervil
**   or tarragon, or 1 teaspoon dried**

½ cup white wine
½ cup water
1 tablespoon Pernod, or anisette liquor
salt
black pepper, freshly ground
1 large lemon, thinly sliced

1 Scale and wash fish, and remove heads and fins.
2 Place in a shallow casserole dish and sprinkle with onions, garlic and herbs.
3 Pour over wine, water and Pernod.
4 Season with salt and pepper.
5 Cover with slices of lemon.
6 Bake in an oven at 180°C (350°F) for approximately 20 minutes or until fish flakes easily with a fork.
7 Baste at intervals during cooking, and if necessary add a little more water and wine.

Whole Fish in Black Bean Sauce

Smoked Cod Provençal

Serves: 4
Cooking time: 30 minutes

775 kJ (185 cal) per serve

750 g (1½ lb) smoked cod
1 large tomato, chopped roughly
1 medium onion, chopped
½ cup dry white wine
250 g (8 oz) fresh mushrooms, peeled and sliced

4 cloves garlic, crushed
pinch thyme
black pepper
salt
4 tablespoons tomato paste

Garnish
parsley, chopped

1 Cut fish into serving pieces and place in a frying pan.
2 Cover fish with cold water. Bring slowly to the boil. Discard water, then add fresh water and bring to the boil again. Drain and keep warm.
3 Add tomato and onion to frying pan. Cook gently for a few minutes, then add wine. Cook mixture until wine has reduced by half.
4 Add mushrooms and garlic. Simmer for 5 minutes. Stir in seasonings and tomato paste.
5 Add fish. Spoon sauce over fish and cook until the mixture is heated through.
6 Garnish with parsley.

Fish Steam Boat

Serves: 4
Cooked at the table in a steam boat or fondue pot

810 kJ (195 cal) per serve

500 g (1 lb) fillets white fish
1 cup soy sauce
2 teaspoons finely chopped green ginger
juice of 1 lemon
185 g (6 oz) silverbeet or spinach

185 g (6 oz) mushrooms
8 spring onions or shallots
185 g (6 oz) bean shoots
1 litre (2 pints) Court Bouillon
  (see page 45)

1 Finely slice fish fillets and marinate for 30 minutes in ½ cup soy sauce, 1 teaspoon ginger and lemon juice.
2 Wash all vegetables.
3 Thinly slice silverbeet and mushrooms and slice the spring onions lengthways and cut into pieces approximately 5 cm (2 in) long.
4 Arrange silverbeet, mushrooms, spring onions, bean shoots and fish on a flat platter.
5 Mix the remaining soy sauce and ginger and place in a small dish.
6 Heat the Court Bouillon, pour into a steam boat or fondue pot and place over a flame on the table.
7 Place the platter containing fish and vegetables and the dish of soy sauce and ginger on the table.
8 Each guest should be given a small bowl, chopsticks and a spoon, or a spoon and fork.
9 Guests select pieces of fish and vegetables and drop these into the hot Court Bouillon to cook quickly for 1-2 minutes.
10 The soy sauce and ginger may be sprinkled over the food when cooked.
Note: The Court Bouillon becomes richer in flavour during the cooking and can be drunk as a soup during the meal. If necessary, more water may be added.

Curried Tuna

Serves: 4
Cooking time: 1-1¼ hours

1175 kJ (280 cal) per serve

2 cups tuna or salmon (in brine)
1 medium carrot
1 small parsnip
1 medium onion
1 medium zucchini
1 stick celery

1 large tomato
1 cup tinned unsweetened apricot
  halves, drained
3 teaspoons curry powder
salt and pepper
1½ cups water

Accompaniments
lemon wedges
tomato wedges

diced cucumber
strips of pawpaw

1 Drain fish and retain juice.
2 Peel carrot, parsnip, onion and zucchini.
3 Roughly chop all vegetables and apricots.
4 Add vegetables, apricots, curry powder, salt, pepper, water and fish juice.
5 Bring to the boil and simmer for 1 hour.
6 Purée in an electric blender or push through a wire sieve, and place back into saucepan.
7 Flake fish and gently fold into the curry sauce.
8 Reheat and serve with bowls of accompaniments.

Tuna Rissoles

Serves: 4
Cooking time: 30 minutes

1485 kJ (355 cal) per serve

250 g (8 oz) pumpkin, peeled
1½ cups chunk style tuna (in brine)
2 egg whites
3 tablespoons chopped fresh parsley
1 medium onion, chopped
1 chicken stock cube, crumbled

½ teaspoon curry powder
garlic salt
4 starch-reduced crispbreads, finely
  crushed
1 tablespoon polyunsaturated margarine
1 tablespoon polyunsaturated oil

Garnish
lemon wedges

1 Cook pumpkin in boiling salted water until soft. Drain and mash.
2 Drain tuna and place in a large mixing bowl.
3 Add egg whites, parsley, onion, stock cube and seasonings.
4 Add mashed pumpkin. Mix well together.
5 Shape into 8 patties. Coat each one lightly with crispbread crumbs.
6 Heat oil and margarine in a large frying pan. Add patties carefully.
7 Cook until browned on both sides (approximately 10 minutes).
8 Serve, garnished with lemon wedges.

Note: The patties should be handled carefully when cooking, as they are soft and tend to break.

Lemon Bream

Serves: 4
Cooking time: 15 minutes

680 kJ (160 cal) per serve

¼ **cup lemon juice**
¼ **cup dry white wine**
6 spring onions or shallots, chopped

pinch black pepper
pinch thyme
750 g (1½ lb) bream fillets, skinned

Garnish
parsley, chopped

1 Put lemon juice, wine, onions and seasonings in a frying pan. Bring to the boil and simmer for 5 minutes or until the liquid has reduced slightly.
2 Place fish fillets in the sauce. Simmer for about 10 minutes or until cooked through. Turn once to ensure even cooking.
3 Remove fish to a heated serving plate, sprinkle with parsley, spoon over sauce, and serve.

Whiting Westernport

Serves: 4
Cooking time: 20 minutes
Oven temperature: 180°C (350°F)

755 kJ (180 cal) per serve

4 fillets whiting, weighing about 750 g
  (1½ lb) in total
1 tablespoon lemon juice
1 cup liquid skim milk

salt and pepper
¼ **teaspoon dried oregano**
6 spring onions or shallots, finely chopped

1 Rub fish with lemon juice and place into a flat casserole dish.
2 Pour over skim milk.
3 Season with salt, pepper and oregano, add spring onions or shallots.
4 Cover the dish and bake in the oven at 180°C (350°F) for 20 minutes.

Grilled Barramundi Steaks

Serves: 4
Cooking time: 10 minutes

785 kJ (190 cal) per serve

1 tablespoon polyunsaturated margarine
4 barramundi steaks, approximately
  185 g (6 oz) each
juice of 1 lemon

2 tablespoons finely chopped fresh chives
salt
black pepper, freshly ground

Garnish
lemon wedges

1 Preheat griller.
2 Place a sheet of aluminium foil on griller tray.
3 Spread half margarine over the foil.
4 Place steaks on greased foil. Turn up edges of foil to retain any juices.
5 Squeeze lemon juice over steaks, sprinkle with chives, salt and freshly ground black pepper.
6 Grill until cooked through.
7 Serve immediately, garnished with lemon wedges.

Fish Capricorn

Serves: 4
Cooking time: 20 minutes

955 kJ (230 cal) per serve

2 teaspoons polyunsaturated oil
750 g (1½ lb) white fish, cut into
   2.5 cm (1 in) pieces
2 cups unsweetened diced pineapple
125 g (4 oz) fresh mushrooms, peeled
   and chopped

2.5 cm (1 in) piece green ginger, thinly
   sliced
2 tablespoons soy sauce
½ green pepper (capsicum), chopped
5-6 drops artificial liquid sweetener

1   Heat oil in a frying pan and add fish. Cook quickly and remove.
2   Clean pan. Add pineapple with juice, mushrooms, ginger and soy sauce. Simmer until liquid has almost evaporated.
3   Add green pepper and cook for a further 5 minutes.
4   Add fish, heat through, and serve.

Poached Fish Lucille

Serves: 4
Cooking time: 30 minutes
Oven temperature: 180°C (350°F)

955 kJ (230 cal) per serve

4 fillets white fish, weighing about 750 g
   (1½ lb) in total
1 tablespoon lemon juice
½ cup skim milk powder

2 cups water
4 egg whites
salt
6 spring onions or shallots, finely chopped

1   Rub fish with lemon juice and place into a flat baking dish.
2   Mix skim milk powder with water.
3   Beat in egg whites and salt.
4   Pour over fish. Add spring onions or shallots.
5   Place dish into a larger dish containing a small amount of cold water and bake in the oven at 180°C (350°F) for 30 minutes or until mixture sets firmly.

Fish in Sweet and Sour Sauce

Serves: 4
Cooking time: 30 minutes
Oven temperature: 180°C (350°F)

885 kJ (210 cal) per serve

4 fillets white fish, weighing about 750 g
   (1½ lb) in total
1 medium white onion
1 small carrot
1 small green pepper (capsicum)
1 stalk celery

½ teaspoon finely chopped green ginger
1 clove garlic, finely chopped
1½ cups unsweetened tomato juice
1 cup unsweetened canned pineapple
   pieces, juice included
salt

1   Place fillets of fish into a flat casserole dish.
2   Dice onion, carrot, pepper and celery and sprinkle over fish.
3   Add ginger, garlic, tomato juice, pineapple and salt.
4   Bake in the oven at 180°C (350°F) for 30 minutes.

Fish Turbans

Serves: 4
Cooking time: 10 minutes
Oven temperature: 200°C (400°F)

780 kJ (185 cal) per serve

8 x 90 g (3 oz) fresh fillets white fish
1 teaspoon dried thyme
1 tablespoon finely chopped fresh parsley
1 tablespoon lemon juice

salt and pepper
90 g (3 oz) smoked salmon, thinly sliced
1 cup Court Bouillon (see page 45)

Garnish
8 capers
8 sprigs parsley

1 Lay fish fillets out flat.
2 Mix thyme, parsley, lemon juice, salt and pepper.
3 Spread herb mixture over fish.
4 Trim salmon into pieces similar in width to the fish fillets and lay flat over the fillets.
5 Roll fish and secure with wooden toothpicks.
6 Stand rolls in a flat baking dish, pour in Court Bouillon, cover and bake in the oven at 200°C (400°F) for 10 minutes.
7 Top each turban with a caper and a sprig of parsley and serve.

Flamed Fish

Serves: 4
Cooking time: 20 minutes
Oven temperature: 180°C (350°F)

610 kJ (145 cal) per serve

4 whole white fish
4 tablespoons finely chopped fresh parsley
1 tablespoon finely chopped fresh thyme, or 1 teaspoon dried
1 tablespoon finely chopped fresh rosemary, or 1 teaspoon dried

salt
black pepper, freshly ground
1 cup water
1 cup dry white wine
3 tablespoons brandy

1 Gut, scale and rinse fish. Remove head and fins.
2 Combine the herbs and place half into the fish cavities.
3 Season with salt and pepper and place the fish under a hot griller for 4 minutes (2 minutes on each side).
4 Transfer to a shallow baking dish, pour over water and wine.
5 Bake in the oven at 180°C (350°F) for approximately 15 minutes or until the fish flakes easily with a fork.
6 Baste the fish at intervals and if necessary add a little more water and wine.
7 Drain fish gently and sprinkle the remainder of the herbs over them.
8 Heat brandy in a spoon, ignite it, pour immediately over the fish. Serve while still flaming.

Salmon Casserole

Serves: 4   *850 kJ (200 cal) per serve*
Cooking time: 30 minutes
Oven temperature: 190°C (375°F)

2 cups salmon (in brine)   ½ teaspoon dried oregano
1 stalk celery, diced   1 medium onion, sliced
1 tablespoon lemon juice   2 medium tomatoes, sliced
salt and pepper   ½ cup tomato juice

1   Remove bones and dark skin from salmon.
2   Gently mix salmon with celery, lemon juice, salt, pepper and oregano.
3   Cook onion slices for 3 minutes in boiling water, drain.
4   Place half of the salmon mixture into a small casserole dish.
5   Cover with onion and tomato slices and top with the remainder of the salmon.
6   Pour tomato juice over fish and bake uncovered in the oven at 190°C (375°F) for 30 minutes.

Salmon Balls

Serves: 4   *855 kJ (205 cal) per serve*
Cooking time: 20 minutes
Oven temperature: 190°C (375°F)

2 cups salmon (in brine)   2 teaspoons lemon juice
315 g (10 oz) pumpkin, peeled   pinch dried oregano
salt   1 egg white
2 teaspoons chopped fresh chives   ¼ teaspoon polyunsaturated oil

1   Remove any dark skin and bones from salmon and drain well.
2   Cut pumpkin into small pieces, cook in boiling salted water until soft, drain well, mash and cool.
3   Combine salmon with pumpkin, salt, chives, lemon juice, oregano and egg white and mix well.
4   Rub a flat biscuit tray with polyunsaturated oil.
5   Roll salmon mixture into small balls and place on the tray.
6   Bake in the oven at 190°C (375°F) for 10 minutes and serve hot.

Javanese Fish

Serves: 4   *690 kJ (165 cal) per serve*
Cooking time: 10 minutes

4 tablespoons soy sauce   grated rind and juice of 1 lemon
2.5 cm (1 in) piece green ginger, sliced   2 tablespoons water
   very thinly   750 g (1½ lb) firm fleshed white fish
2 garlic cloves, crushed

Garnish
lemon slices

1   Combine all ingredients except fish.
2   Pour over fish and marinate for at least 2 hours.
3   Grill fish, spooning marinade over frequently to prevent drying.
4   Serve garnished with lemon slices.

Fish Baked in Tomato Juice

Serves: 4
Cooking time: 15 minutes
Oven temperature: 180°C (350°F)

710 kJ (170 cal) per serve

4 fillets white fish
juice of 1 lemon
¼ teaspoon dried oregano

salt
black pepper, freshly ground
1½ cups tomato juice

Garnish
1 tablespoon finely chopped fresh parsley

1 Place fish into a flat casserole dish.
2 Sprinkle with lemon juice, oregano, salt and pepper.
3 Pour over tomato juice and cover.
4 Bake in the oven at 180°C (350°F) for 15 minutes.
5 Sprinkle with parsley and serve.

Waitangi Whiting

Serves: 4
Cooking time: 10 minutes
Oven temperature: 180°C (350°F)

745 kJ (180 cal) per serve

4 fillets whiting, about 750 g (1½ lb) in total
1 tablespoon lemon juice
1 kiwi fruit (Chinese gooseberry)

salt and pepper
1 cup liquid skim milk
1 teaspoon finely chopped fresh parsley

1 Wash fillets and rub with lemon juice.
2 Peel kiwi fruit and quarter lengthwise.
3 Place 1 piece of kiwi fruit across each fillet of fish.
4 Roll up and secure with wooden toothpicks.
5 Place in a flat baking dish and sprinkle with salt and pepper.
6 Pour over skim milk, cover and bake in the oven at 180°C (350°F) for 10 minutes.
7 Remove toothpicks, sprinkle with chopped parsley and serve hot.

Fish Mexicano

Serves: 4
Cooking time: 45 minutes
Oven temperature: 180°C (350°F)

770 kJ (185 cal) per serve

4 fillets white fish (bream, flathead or whiting), weighing about 750 g (1½ lb) in total
1 medium onion, chopped
salt
black pepper

½ teaspoon dried basil
½ cup chopped green pepper (capsicum)
1 x 140 g can tomato paste
4 cloves garlic, crushed
4-6 drops chilli sauce
1 cup water

1 Preheat oven to 180°C (350°F).
2 Place fish in an ovenproof casserole.
3 Combine all other ingredients in a saucepan. Bring to the boil and simmer for 10 minutes.
4 Check flavour, pour over fish, and bake uncovered for 30 minutes.

POULTRY AND GAME

Chicken, turkey and rabbit are low in saturated fats.

Chicken can be cooked in an infinite variety of ways, and, therefore it can be served at least twice a week without repetition. Boned breast of chicken is the part lowest in fat content, so we have used this in many of our recipes.

Some cooking hints:

- Poultry has a layer of fat under the skin and several fat deposits near the tail. When cooking a whole chicken remove as much of this fat as possible. Alternatively, remove all the skin and fat, and place the bird in an oven bag with a marinade to keep the flesh moist.
- Individual chicken pieces may be skinned before or after cooking. We recommend leaving the skin on until ready to serve to prevent the meat from drying out.
- Rabbit can be substituted for chicken in the recipes in this section.
- We have allowed 185 g (6 oz) per serve for all chicken and rabbit recipes. As turkey is higher in fat, we have reduced the size of each serve to 125 g (4 oz).

Chicken à la Grecque (page 110)

Lemon Chicken in Foil

Serves: 4
Cooking time: 1 hour
Oven temperature: 180°C (350°F)

1210 kJ (290 cal) per serve

1 x No.13 (1.3 kg) chicken
2 teaspoons polyunsaturated margarine
salt and pepper

juice and rind of 1 lemon
2 cloves garlic, crushed
1 tablespoon soy sauce

1 Joint chicken and remove skin and visible fat.
2 Heat margarine in a frying pan and fry chicken until brown.
3 Place a sheet of aluminium foil on a baking tray. Place the chicken on this and sprinkle with salt and pepper.
4 Mix lemon juice, lemon rind, garlic and soy sauce and pour over chicken. Wrap chicken, making sure the package is sealed well.
5 Bake for 1 hour at 180°C (350°F).

Chicken Saté

Serves: 4
Cooking time: 5 minutes

905 kJ (215 cal) per serve

500 g (1 lb) boned chicken
1 clove garlic, crushed
2 tablespoons lemon juice

1 small onion, grated
salt
1 teaspoon polyunsaturated oil

Sauce
½ cup soy sauce
½ teaspoon dried chilli powder (or according to taste)

1 teaspoon lemon juice
¼ teaspoon crushed garlic
¼ teaspoon finely chopped green ginger

1 Cut chicken into 1 cm (½ in) cubes.
2 Thread onto skewers (approximately 5 cubes per skewer).
3 Marinate in the remaining ingredients (except sauce) for at least 1 hour, turning at intervals.
4 Grill over a charcoal fire, or under a griller, turning frequently and basting occasionally with the marinade.
5 Combine all the sauce ingredients, mixing well, and serve as a dunking sauce.

Chicken Charmaine

Serves: 4
Cooking time: 45 minutes
Oven temperature: 190°C (375°F)

1220 kJ (290 cal) per serve

1 x No.13 (1.3 kg) chicken
2 cloves garlic, finely chopped
1 tablespoon dry sherry

1 tablespoon soy sauce
salt
1 bunch leeks, sliced

1 Remove skin and all visible fat from the chicken.
2 Combine the garlic, sherry, soy sauce and salt. Add the leeks to *half* of this sauce.
3 Fill the chicken cavity with the leek mixture. Sew and truss the chicken.
4 Rub the remaining sauce over the chicken.
5 Place chicken into an oven bag and tie.
6 Place in a baking dish and bake for 45 minutes.
7 Cut chicken into serving pieces and serve with the leeks and juices.

Chicken Saté

Roast Chicken in Special Sauce

Serves: 4
Cooking time: 30 minutes
Oven temperature: 220°C (425°F)

1230 kJ (295 cal) per serve

1 x No.13 (1.3 kg) chicken
2 tablespoons dry sherry
2 tablespoons soy sauce
2 tablespoons lemon juice
½ teaspoon monosodium glutamate

salt
1 teaspoon finely chopped green ginger
1 clove garlic, finely chopped
2 teaspoons polyunsaturated oil

Garnish
2 teaspoons finely chopped fresh parsley

1 Remove skin and all visible fat from chicken, cut into serving-size pieces and place in a shallow baking dish.
2 Mix all other ingredients together to make a marinade and pour over the chicken pieces.
3 Marinate the chicken for at least 30 minutes.
4 Roast in the oven at 220°C (425°F) for 30 minutes, turning and basting chicken at intervals.
5 Sprinkle with parsley and serve.

Waianae Chicken

Serves: 6
Cooking time: 1½ hours

1520 kJ (365 cal) per serve

1 x No.15 (1.5 kg) boiling chicken
1 large onion, sliced
1 large carrot, sliced
2 stalks celery, chopped
¼ teaspoon mixed dried herbs
6 peppercorns

salt
1½ cups water
1½ cups dry white wine
1 whole pineapple
½ cup skim milk powder
pinch saffron or turmeric

Garnish
1 teaspoon finely chopped fresh parsley

1 Place chicken in a large saucepan with onion, carrot, celery, herbs, peppercorns, salt, water and wine.
2 Bring to the boil, reduce heat and simmer for approximately 1½ hours.
3 Drain the liquid and skim off the fat.
4 Skin and bone the chicken, cut the meat into bite-size pieces and return to clean saucepan.
5 Add the carrot to the chicken and discard other vegetables.
6 Slice the pineapple and its top in half, lengthwise.
7 Scoop out the flesh, cut it into bite-size pieces and add it to the chicken.
8 Place the pineapple shells in a warm oven to heat.
9 Mix 1 cup of the stock with the skim milk powder and mix with the chicken, carrot and pineapple.
10 Colour a pale yellow with the saffron or turmeric.
11 Heat and spoon into pineapple shells.
12 Sprinkle with parsley and serve.

Chicken Tandoori

Serves: 4
Cooking time: 1 hour 10 minutes
Oven temperature: 180°C (350°F)

1170 kJ (280 cal) per serve

1 x No.13 (1.3 kg) chicken
½ cup non-fat natural yoghurt
½ teaspoon ground ginger
½ teaspoon cinnamon
grated rind of 1 lemon

1 clove garlic, crushed
pinch five-spice powder
juice of ½ lemon
2 spring onions or shallots, finely chopped

1 Joint and skin chicken. Remove any visible fat. Place in a large mixing bowl.
2 Mix remaining ingredients and spoon over chicken. Mix well.
3 Cover and refrigerate for 4-5 hours.
4 Heat oven to 180°C (350°F). Place chicken pieces and marinade in a baking dish. Cover with aluminium foil. Bake for 30 minutes.
5 Remove foil and allow chicken to cook for a further 30 minutes.
6 Take chicken out of the oven. Heat the griller. Lift chicken pieces onto a shallow tray and grill until well browned on all sides. Serve.

Chicken with Champignons

Serves: 4
Cooking time: 25 minutes

1480 kJ (355 cal) per serve

1 x No.13 (1.3 kg) chicken
salt
1 tablespoon polyunsaturated oil
12 spring onions or shallots,
   finely chopped
2 cloves garlic, crushed

3 tablespoons soy sauce
2 tablespoons dry sherry
1 teaspoon finely sliced fresh ginger
½ cup unsweetened tomato juice
1 cup drained, canned
   champignons

Garnish
1 tablespoon chopped fresh parsley

1 Remove skin and all visible fat from chicken. Remove meat from carcass, cut into bite-size pieces. Sprinkle with salt.
2 Heat oil in a frying pan or wok. Add chicken, spring onions or shallots and garlic, and fry until well browned. Remove.
3 Drain any oil from the pan and wipe with a paper towel.
4 Add soy sauce, sherry, ginger and tomato juice. Simmer gently for 5 minutes.
5 Add champignons and chicken and simmer for 5 minutes or until liquid has reduced and thickened. Garnish with parsley, and serve.

Chicken Napoleon

Serves: 4
Cooking time: 1 hour   *1345 kJ (320 cal) per serve*

1 x No.13 (1.3 kg) chicken
2 teaspoons polyunsaturated margarine
3 tablespoons brandy
3 tablespoons chopped fresh chives
3 tablespoons chopped fresh parsley
½ cup dry white wine

pinch dried thyme
salt
black pepper
2 medium zucchini, sliced
250 g (8 oz) baby carrots, peeled
2 tablespoons non-fat natural yoghurt

Garnish
parsley, chopped

1 Cut chicken into serving pieces, removing skin and visible fat.
2 Heat margarine in a frying pan. Add chicken and brown well on all sides.
3 Remove chicken, wipe out the pan to remove excess fat. Return chicken and slowly reheat.
4 Pour in brandy and ignite.
5 Add chives, parsley, wine and seasonings. Spoon chicken and sauce into a saucepan. Cover and simmer gently for 30 minutes.
6 Add zucchini and baby carrots, and continue cooking until chicken and vegetables are tender.
7 Lift chicken pieces onto a serving dish and keep hot.
8 Boil sauce until reduced. Remove from heat.
9 Stir yoghurt to remove lumps and fold into sauce. Pour over chicken and serve, garnished with parsley.

Coq au Vin

Serves: 4
Cooking time: 1 hour
Oven temperature: 160°C (325°F)   *1195 kJ (285 cal) per serve*

1 x No.13 (1.3 kg) chicken
3 tablespoons brandy
2 medium white onions
2 cloves garlic
2 large sprigs each of parsley and thyme
2 bay leaves

salt
black pepper, freshly ground
1 cup dry red wine
125 g (4 oz) fresh button mushrooms or champignons

Garnish
2 tablespoons finely chopped fresh parsley

1 Cut chicken into serving-size pieces and remove skin and all visible fat.
2 Place into a fireproof casserole, pour over brandy, toss the chicken, heat, ignite and let the flame burn out.
3 Roughly chop each onion into 8 large pieces.
4 Add the onion, garlic, parsley, thyme, bay leaves, salt, pepper, and wine to the casserole.
5 Stir, cover and bring to the boil. Reduce heat and add mushrooms.
6 Simmer on top of the stove or in the oven at 160°C (325°F) for approximately 1 hour.
7 Remove the herbs and serve, sprinkled with parsley.

100

Summer Chicken

Serves: 6
Cooking time: 1½ hours

1140 kJ (370 cal) per serve

1 x No.15 (1.5 kg) boiling chicken
1 large onion
1 large carrot
2 stalks celery
salt and pepper
¼ teaspoon mixed dried herbs

1½ cups water
1½ cups dry white wine
1 tablespoon green peas, cooked
3 hard-boiled eggs, whites only
1 tablespoon gelatine

Garnish
3 lettuce leaves, finely shredded

1 Place the chicken into a large saucepan.
2 Slice onion and carrot into rings, chop celery and add to the saucepan.
3 Add salt, pepper, herbs, water and wine.
4 Bring to the boil, reduce the heat and simmer for approximately 1½ hours or until tender.
5 Drain off the liquid, cool and remove the fat from the stock.
6 Skin and bone the chicken and pass the meat through a mincer or chop finely.
7 Melt the stock over heat, add gelatine and dissolve. Pour a thin layer into the base of a 1-litre (2-pint) mould.
8 Arrange some of the carrot rings and the peas into a pattern on the base of the mould and place in a refrigerator to set.
9 Finely chop the remaining carrot and egg white and mix through the meat.
10 Stir in the remaining stock, spoon into the mould, press firmly and place in the refrigerator to set.
11 Carefully and quickly heat the base and sides of the mould by plunging it into hot water. Turn the chicken mould out, upside down, onto a flat platter.
12 Serve chilled, surrounded by a bed of shredded lettuce.

Chicken Skewers

Serves: 4
Cooking time: 20 minutes

820 kJ (195 cal) per serve

4 chicken breasts, skinned
1 tablespoon lemon juice
½ teaspoon ground ginger
¼ teaspoon cayenne pepper
½ teaspoon dry mustard
¼ teaspoon turmeric

1 teaspoon curry powder
2 tablespoons non-fat natural yoghurt
salt
1 teaspoon Worcestershire sauce
2 teaspoons tomato paste
1 large onion, cut into wedges

1 Cut chicken into 5 cm (2 in) pieces and sprinkle with lemon juice. Place in a mixing bowl.
2 Mix ginger, cayenne, mustard, turmeric, curry powder, yoghurt, salt, Worcestershire sauce and tomato paste to a smooth paste. Pour over chicken. Stir well, cover and marinate for 1 hour in the refrigerator.
3 Thread chicken and onion wedges on 4 skewers.
4 Heat griller. Grill chicken slowly, turning frequently until cooked.

Chicken and Asparagus Cream

Serves: 4
Cooking time: 50 minutes
Oven temperature: 180°C (350°F)

1385 kJ (330 cal) per serve

1 x No.13 (1.3 kg) chicken
2 cups water
2 stalks celery, roughly chopped
1 medium carrot, roughly chopped
1 medium onion, roughly chopped

salt and pepper
pinch mixed dried herbs
1½ cups drained asparagus cuts
2 tablespoons skim milk powder
2 egg whites

1 Place chicken in a saucepan with water, celery, carrot, onion, salt, pepper and herbs.
2 Simmer for 30 minutes and remove chicken.
3 Skin, bone and dice chicken, removing all visible fat.
4 Drain and skim fat from chicken stock.
5 Place chicken in a casserole dish.
6 Lay asparagus across the chicken.
7 Beat 1 cup stock with skim milk powder and egg whites.
8 Pour over chicken and asparagus and bake in the oven at 180°C (350°F) for 20 minutes or until set.

Note: Do not overcook chicken as mixture will separate.

Chicken Valencia

Serves: 4
Cooking time: 1¼ hours
Oven temperature: 180°C (350 °F)

1420 kJ (340 cal) per serve

1 x No.13 (1.3 kg) chicken
salt and pepper
2 teaspoons polyunsaturated oil
1 cup orange juice
1 cup drained, canned
  champignons

1 tablespoon soy sauce
½ teaspoon garlic salt
½ cup dry white wine
1 orange, sliced

Garnish
parsley

1   Joint chicken, removing skin and visible fat. Sprinkle lightly with salt and pepper.
2   Heat oil in a frying pan. Fry chicken until brown, then place in an ovenproof casserole.
3   Add orange juice to pan, then champignons, soy sauce, garlic salt and wine. Simmer until reduced to half.
4   Place orange slices over chicken in casserole.
5   Pour sauce over chicken. Cover casserole and bake in the oven at 180°C (350°F) for 1 hour or until chicken is tender.
6   Remove from oven. Garnish with parsley and serve.

Silver and Jade

Serves: 4
Cooking time: 12-15 minutes

1465 kJ (350 cal) per serve

375 g (12 oz) fresh or frozen broccoli
salt
500 g (1 lb) boned uncooked chicken meat
250 g (8 oz) veal cutlets

1 tablespoon polyunsaturated oil
¼ cup water
1 chicken stock cube

1   Wash broccoli and remove coarse leaves and woody sections of stalks. Drop into boiling, salted water.
2   Boil for 6-8 minutes, drain and cut into pieces 5 cm (2 in) long.
3   Remove all visible fat from the chicken and veal and cut into pieces 2.5 cm x 1 cm x 1 cm (1 in x ½ in x ½ in).
4   Heat oil in a wok or large frying pan and quickly fry meat until tender (approximately 6 minutes), tossing continually.
5   Add water, stock cube and broccoli. Toss gently, reheat and serve as soon as possible.

Southern Barbecued Chicken

Serves: 4
Cooking time: 1 hour
Oven temperature: 180°C (350°F)

1165 kJ (280 cal) per serve

1 x No.13 (1.3 kg) chicken
4 tablespoons tomato paste
¼ cup vinegar
½ teaspoon monosodium glutamate
½ teaspoon garlic salt

black pepper
1 tablespoon Worcestershire sauce
2-3 drops artificial sweetener
1 teaspoon dry mustard

1 Line a baking dish with aluminium foil.
2 Cut chicken into serving pieces, removing skin and all visible fat. Place in a baking dish and fold edges of foil over to hold marinade.
3 Mix all other ingredients together.
4 Pour half the marinade over the chicken. Bake for 30 minutes at 180°C (350°F), then remove from oven and pour off excess juices. Pour remainder of marinade over chicken and return to the oven for a further 30 minutes.

Chicken Chow Mein

Serves: 4
Cooking time: 10 minutes

1135 kJ (270 cal) per serve

375 g (12 oz) boned chicken meat
185 g (6 oz) veal cutlets
salt
pinch monosodium glutamate
1 teaspoon soy sauce
1 teaspoon brandy

1 clove garlic, finely chopped
2 teaspoons polyunsaturated oil
2 cups finely shredded cabbage
1 cup finely chopped celery
2 tablespoons water
8 spring onions or shallots, finely chopped

1 Remove all visible fat from the chicken and veal, and cut into pieces 2.5 cm x 1 cm x 1 cm (1 in x ½ in x ½ in).
2 Mix the salt, monosodium glutamate, soy sauce, brandy and garlic with the meat and marinate for at least ½ hour.
3 Heat the oil in a wok or a large frying pan and quickly fry the meat until tender (approximately 6 minutes), tossing continually.
4 Remove from the pan.
5 Add cabbage, celery and water to the pan, toss well. Cover and cook for 5 minutes, tossing occasionally.
6 Return meat to the pan, add spring onions or shallots and mix.
7 Check seasoning, reheat and serve.

Chicken in Vermouth

Serves: 4
Cooking time: 1 hour
Oven temperature: 180°C (350°F)

1095 kJ (260 cal) per serve

1 x No.13 (1.3 kg) chicken
1 chicken stock cube

½ cup water
½ cup dry vermouth

Garnish
1 tablespoon finely chopped fresh chives

1   Remove skin and visible fat from chicken. Cut chicken into serving pieces.
2   Dissolve stock cube in water, pour into frying pan and add chicken pieces. Cook chicken until well browned on both sides, turning frequently to avoid burning. Allow stock to boil away completely.
3   Add vermouth and simmer gently for 5 minutes.
4   Place chicken and sauce into ovenproof casserole and bake in the oven for 30 minutes at 180°C (350°F).
5   Serve, garnished with chives.

Chicken Citrus

Serves: 4
Cooking time: 35 minutes
Oven temperature: 220°C (425°F)

1135 kJ (270 cal) per serve

1 x No.13 (1.3 kg) chicken
1 tablespoon soy sauce
1 lemon, sliced
1 tablespoon dry sherry

2 cups water
1 chicken stock cube
salt and pepper

Garnish
2 teaspoons finely chopped fresh parsley
1 lemon, cut into wedges

1   Remove skin and all visible fat from chicken and rub with soy sauce.
2   Thinly slice lemon and soak this in sherry for 5 minutes.
3   Place chicken in an ovenproof casserole and cover with lemon slices.
4   Pour water around chicken, crumble in stock cube and season with salt and pepper.
5   Cover and bake at 220°C (425°F) for 30 minutes or until tender.
6   Discard lemon, cut chicken into serving-size pieces and grill quickly under a hot griller until slightly browned.
7   Reduce sauce over heat, pour over chicken pieces, sprinkle with parsley, decorate with lemon wedges and serve.

Almond Chicken

Serves: 4
Cooking time: 1 hour
Oven temperature: 180°C (350°F)

1355 kJ (325 cal) per serve

1 x No.13 (1.3 kg) chicken
1 tablespoon polyunsaturated margarine
2 cloves garlic, crushed

15 g (½ oz) ground almonds
1 tablespoon chopped fresh chives
salt and pepper

1   Skin, joint and remove any visible fat from chicken. Place pieces in a shallow baking dish or casserole.
2   Melt margarine in a saucepan, add crushed garlic.
3   Brush margarine and garlic mixture over chicken pieces.
4   Sprinkle almonds and chives over chicken pieces then sprinkle lightly with salt and pepper.
5   Bake uncovered in a moderate oven at 180°C (350°F) for 1 hour or until cooked.

Chicken Pillows

Serves: 4
Cooking time: 1¼ hours
Oven temperature: 180°C (350°F)

915 kJ (220 cal) per serve

4 whole chicken breasts, boned
250 g (8 oz) fresh mushrooms, peeled and finely chopped
1 tablespoon chopped fresh chives
½ cup finely chopped celery
½ cup dry white wine
salt and pepper

2 teaspoons polyunsaturated oil
¾ cup dry white wine
1 tablespoon chopped fresh parsley
½ cup water
1 chicken stock cube
salt and pepper
2 tablespoons non-fat natural yoghurt

Garnish
parsley, chopped

1   Remove skin from chicken breasts. Pound meat lightly to flatten.
2   Place mushrooms in a frying pan with chives, celery, wine and seasonings. Simmer until the liquid has evaporated.
3   Divide mixture into 4 and spread on chicken breasts. Roll up carefully and secure with string.
4   Fry chicken in oil until golden brown on all sides. Place in an ovenproof casserole.
5   Add wine, parsley, water, stock cube, salt and pepper to the frying pan and bring to the boil. Reduce slightly, then pour over chicken. Cover and bake in the oven for 1 hour at 180°C (350°F).
6   Drain liquid from casserole into a saucepan, return chicken to oven to keep hot. Boil liquid until reduced by half. Remove from heat, stir in yoghurt.
7   Pour sauce over chicken, garnish with parsley and serve.

Golden Chicken

Serves: 4
Cooking time: 1½ hours
Oven temperature: 180°C (350°F)

1445 kJ (345 cal) per serve

2 cups drained unsweetened apricots
1 x No.13 (1.3 kg) chicken
2 teaspoons polyunsaturated margarine

1 large onion, chopped
salt
black pepper

Garnish
parsley or chives, chopped

1   Puree apricots in an electric blender or push through a sieve.
2   Skin and joint chicken. Remove any visible fat from meat.
3   Melt margarine in a frying pan. Add chicken pieces and brown on all sides. Remove to a covered ovenproof casserole.
4   Add onion to the frying pan and cook until clear. Add to chicken. Sprinkle salt and pepper over chicken.
5   Pour purée over meat. Cover and cook in moderate oven at 180°C (350°F) for 45 minutes or until tender.
6   When chicken is cooked, remove from the oven and drain sauce off into a saucepan. Cover chicken and keep hot. Reduce sauce by boiling until thick.
7   Pour sauce over chicken, sprinkle with parsley or chives and serve.

Chicken à La Grecque

Serves: 4
Cooking time: 45 minutes
Oven temperature: 190°C (375°F)

1190 kJ (285 cal) per serve

1 x No.13 (1.3 kg) chicken
2 tablespoons paprika
juice of 1 lemon
2 large tomatoes, diced
1 tablespoon tomato paste

2 cloves garlic, finely chopped
¼ teaspoon ground oregano
salt
black pepper, freshly ground
1 bacon stock cube

1   Remove all visible fat from chicken, sprinkle over paprika.
2   Mix lemon juice, tomatoes, tomato paste, garlic, oregano, salt, pepper and stock cube together.
3   Toss chicken in tomato mixture and place it in an oven bag.
4   Spoon any remaining tomato mixture over chicken and secure the bag.
5   Cook in the oven at 190°C (375°F) for 45 minutes.

Brandied Chicken

Serves: 4
Cooking time: 1 hour

1205 kJ (290 cal) per serve

1 x No.13 (1.3 kg) chicken
2 teaspoons polyunsaturated margarine
125 g (4 oz) fresh mushrooms, peeled
  and chopped

salt and pepper
½ cup brandy

1 Skin and joint chicken, removing all visible fat from meat.
2 Heat margarine in a frying pan. Brown chicken on all sides. Remove and place in a heavy saucepan.
3 Brown mushrooms in the frying pan, add salt and pepper. Pour brandy over, ignite and allow alcohol to burn off. Pour mushrooms and liquid over chicken. Cover and simmer gently for 45 minutes.
4 Place chicken on a serving dish, cover and keep hot.
5 Reduce liquid by boiling for 5 minutes, then pour sauce over chicken and serve.

Poulet Zenica

Serves: 4
Cooking time: 1½ hours
Oven temperature: 180°C (350°F)

1325 kJ (315 cal) per serve

1 x No.13 (1.3 kg) chicken
2 teaspoons polyunsaturated margarine
1 medium onion, chopped
2 tablespoons sweet paprika
2 cups chopped tomatoes
4 cloves garlic, crushed

1 chicken stock cube
½ cup water
salt
black pepper
1 tablespoon vinegar

Garnish
parsley, chopped

1 Joint chicken, remove skin and visible fat.
2 Heat margarine in a frying pan. Add chicken and brown slowly. Add onion and cook until clear.
3 Remove chicken and onion to an ovenproof casserole.
4 Add paprika, tomatoes, garlic, stock cube and water, salt, pepper and vinegar to pan. Turn up heat and cook rapidly until mixture thickens.
5 Pour sauce over chicken, cover casserole and bake for 1 hour at 180°C (350°F).
6 Serve, garnished with parsley.

Chicken Marengo

Serves: 4
Cooking time: 1½ hours
Oven temperature: 180°C (350°F)

1345 kJ (320 cal) per serve

1 x No.13 (1.3 kg) chicken
2 teaspoons polyunsaturated oil
1 onion, sliced
¼ green pepper (capsicum), sliced
¼ red pepper (capsicum), sliced
2 tomatoes, roughly chopped
½ cup sliced mushrooms

½ cup water
1 chicken stock cube
½ cup dry white wine
¼ teaspoon dried thyme
¼ teaspoon dried oregano
salt and pepper
2 tablespoons tomato paste

1   Joint chicken, removing skin and all visible fat.
2   Heat oil in a frying pan. Add chicken and brown on all sides. Add onion and cook until clear.
3   Place in an ovenproof casserole.
4   Add vegetables to pan and brown. Spoon into casserole.
5   Mix water, stock cube and wine. Pour into pan and bring to the boil. Add seasonings and tomato paste. Pour over chicken and vegetables.
6   Cover casserole and bake in the oven at 180°C (350°F) for 1 hour or until chicken is tender.

Curried Chicken

Serves: 4
Cooking time: 1 hour
Oven temperature: 180°C (350°F)

1500 kJ (355 cal) per serve

1 x No.13 (1.3 kg) chicken
1 tablespoon polyunsaturated oil
1 medium onion, chopped
½ cup chopped celery
1 medium carrot, peeled and chopped
1 medium apple, peeled, cored and diced
1 tablespoon curry powder

300 ml (10 fl. oz) Chicken Stock (see page 45)
3 tablespoons tomato paste
2 teaspoons lemon juice
salt and pepper
2 tablespoons non-fat natural yoghurt

1   Skin chicken and remove all visible fat. Remove flesh from carcass and dice into 2.5 cm (1 in) pieces.
2   Heat oil in a frying pan. Add onion, celery, carrot and apple and fry until brown. Place in an ovenproof casserole.
3   Add chicken to pan, fry lightly. Remove to casserole. Add curry powder and fry, stirring well.
4   Mix stock, tomato paste, lemon juice, salt and pepper, and pour into pan and bring to the boil. Reduce liquid by half, pour over chicken. Cover and bake for 1 hour in the oven at 180°C (350°F).
5   Allow to cool slightly, then stir in yoghurt and mix through. Serve immediately.

Chicken Malay

Serves: 4
Cooking time: 40 minutes

1280 kJ (305 cal) per serve

1 x No.13 (1.3 kg) chicken
2 cups water
salt
3 medium onions, grated
2 medium tomatoes, peeled and chopped
2 cloves garlic, crushed

pinch ground cinnamon
pinch ground cloves
salt
black pepper, freshly ground
2 tablespoons soy sauce

1. Cut chicken into serving-size pieces, remove skin and all visible fat.
2. Place chicken in a saucepan with water and salt and simmer for 30 minutes.
3. Drain juice and skim off fat.
4. Place the onions, tomatoes, garlic, cinnamon, cloves, salt, pepper, soy sauce and 4 tablespoons of the chicken stock into a clean saucepan.
5. Bring to the boil, drop in the chicken pieces and simmer for 10 minutes. Serve.

Chicken en Cocotte

Serves: 4
Cooking time: 1 hour

1435 kJ (320 cal) per serve

1 x No.13 (1.3 kg) chicken
3 tablespoons brandy
½ bunch spring onions or 6 shallots
2 medium carrots, sliced
4 medium tomatoes, roughly chopped

2 large sprigs each of parsley and thyme
2 bay leaves
1 cup dry red wine
salt
black pepper, freshly ground

1. Cut chicken into serving-size pieces and remove skin and all visible fat.
2. Place into an ovenproof casserole, pour over brandy, toss the chicken, heat, ignite and let the flame burn out.
3. Chop the spring onions and retain the white and green portions separately.
4. Add the white sections of spring onions, carrot, tomato, parsley, thyme, bay leaves, wine, salt and pepper to the casserole.
5. Stir, bring to the boil, reduce heat and simmer for approximately 1 hour or until chicken is tender. Remove herbs.
6. Stir in green sections of spring onions and serve.

Rabbit Bouillabaisse

Serves: 4
Cooking time: 1¼-1½ hours

1360 kJ (325 cal) per serve

1 rabbit, jointed
pinch saffron or turmeric
2 tablespoons Pernod, or anisette liquor
salt
black pepper, freshly ground
2 onions, chopped

2 cloves garlic, finely chopped
2 cups chopped, peeled tomatoes
6 parsley sprigs, finely chopped
1 small head fennel (white part only), chopped
1 cup water

1   Soak rabbit in lukewarm water for 30 minutes. Remove and pat dry.
2   Mix saffron, Pernod, salt, pepper, onions, garlic, tomatoes, parsley and fennel together, pour over the rabbit and stand for 30 minutes.
3   Add water, cover, bring to the boil. Reduce the heat and simmer for 1¼-1½ hours, or until rabbit is tender.

Rabbit in Cider

Serves: 4
Cooking time: 1½ hours

1425 kJ (340 cal) per serve

1 rabbit, jointed
1 tablespoon lemon juice
1 tablespoon polyunsaturated oil
1 large onion, sliced
pinch dried thyme

pinch dried basil
black pepper
salt
1½ cups dry cider
1 tablespoon tomato paste

Garnish
parsley, chopped

1   Soak rabbit for approximately 30 minutes in lukewarm water to which lemon juice has been added.
2   Remove rabbit from water and pat dry.
3   Heat oil and fry rabbit until golden brown. Remove rabbit and place in a heavy saucepan.
4   Fry onion until soft, then add to the meat with the spices.
5   Add cider and tomato paste. Bring to the boil, then cover and simmer gently for 1½ hours. Remove lid, boil rapidly for 5 minutes to reduce liquid.
6   Serve, garnished with parsley.

Summer Chicken (page 102)

Braised Rabbit

Serves: 4
Cooking time: 1 hour

1410 kJ (335 cal) per serve

1 rabbit, jointed
1 tablespoon polyunsaturated oil
1 large onion, sliced

2 bacon stock cubes
2 cups water
salt and pepper

1 Soak rabbit in lukewarm water for 30 minutes. Remove and pat dry.
2 Heat oil in a large frying pan. Cook onion until soft.
3 Drain and remove onion.
4 Brown the rabbit in remaining oil.
5 Return onion to the pan, add stock cubes, water, salt and pepper and bring to the boil.
6 Reduce heat, cover and simmer for approximately 1 hour.

Rabbit Maréchal

Serves: 4
Cooking time: approximately 2 hours

1355 kJ (325 cal) per serve

1 rabbit, jointed
1 medium onion
1 medium carrot
2 stalks celery
2 bay leaves
6 peppercorns

3 sage leaves
2 bacon stock cubes
3 cups water
salt
2 tablespoons skim milk powder
2 tablespoons chopped fresh parsley

1 Soak rabbit in lukewarm water for 30 minutes. Remove and pat dry.
2 Roughly chop onion, carrot and celery and add to rabbit.
3 Add bay leaves, peppercorns, sage, stock cubes, water and salt.
4 Bring to the boil and simmer for approximately 2 hours or until tender.
5 Remove bay leaves, peppercorns and sage.
6 Drain off the liquid and mix it with the skim milk powder.
7 Return liquid to the saucepan and reheat without boiling. Stir in parsley. Serve.

Turkey Divan

Serves: 4
Cooking time: 45 minutes
Oven temperature: 180°C (350°F)

1680 kJ (400 cal) per serve

1 kg (2 lb) fresh asparagus
500 g (1 lb) cooked turkey meat, sliced
¾ cup water

3 chicken stock cubes
¼ cup dry white wine
1 egg yolk, beaten

1 Wash asparagus, snap off woody end and scrape white part of stalk with a knife to remove outer layer.
2 Cook asparagus in boiling, salted water until tender, drain and spread over the base of a shallow ovenproof casserole.
3 Lay turkey slices over asparagus, moisten with a few drops of water, cover and cook in the oven at 180°C (350°F) for 20 minutes.
4 Add stock cubes and wine to water in a saucepan. Bring to the boil and allow to reduce slightly. Reduce heat and simmer gently.
5 Add 2-3 tablespoons stock to the beaten egg yolk, then pour the mixture into the stock, stirring constantly. Stir until slightly thickened.
6 Remove turkey from oven, pour sauce over, then return to the oven for a few minutes to allow flavours to blend, before serving.

Turkey and Ginger Sauce

Serves: 4
Cooking time: 1 hour

1660 kJ (395 cal) per serve

1 large onion
1 large carrot
2 medium cooking apples
3 cups water
2 chicken stock cubes

1 teaspoon finely chopped green ginger
2 teaspoons curry powder
salt and pepper
500 g (1 lb) cooked turkey meat, sliced

1 Peel and roughly chop onion, carrot and apples and place into a saucepan.
2 Add water, stock cubes, ginger, curry powder, salt and pepper.
3 Bring to the boil, reduce the heat and simmer for 45 minutes.
4 Purée the mixture in a blender, or push through a wire sieve.
5 Place turkey into the saucepan and cover with the puréed sauce.
6 Reheat and serve.

BEEF, LAMB AND VEAL

Careful selection and preparation of meats will enable you to eliminate a reasonable amount of fat, particularly saturated fats, and cholesterol from the diet.

Red meats contain greater amounts of animal fat than either fish or chicken; therefore, we suggest that you limit the use of beef or lamb to about three meals a week. Veal is lower in fat than most other meats and can be used more frequently.

Various cooking methods can be applied to minimise the amount of fat in the meat dish before it is finally served:

- Use a rack when grilling, roasting or baking so that fats may drain off.
- Wine, tomato juice and stock serve as flavourful marinades for basting and keeping meats moist during slow cooking.
- Casseroles, stews and stocks are best cooked the day before use and stored in the refrigerator overnight. The solid fats are then easily removed before reheating and serving.
- 'Dry-frying' is a method of browning meat without fat. The secret of dry-frying is to heat the frypan slowly and to turn the meat frequently to avoid burning. Most meat cuts contain sufficient fat to allow this type of cooking.
- An alternative method of browning meat before combining it with other ingredients, is to grill the meat quickly for approximately 5 minutes on each side.
- Gravy *au jus* (meat juices only) can be made by removing the fat from pan drippings. After roasting the meat, pour the drippings into a bowl and stand it in the freezer for 10 minutes. Return the meat to the oven to keep warm. (The meat will also 'set' in this time, and make carving easier.) Skim the fat from the meat drippings and return the liquid to a saucepan to reheat. The gravy may be diluted with water before serving.
- Red meats have a higher fat content than white meats, so we have limited servings of red meat to 125 g (4 oz) per person. We have allowed 185 g (6 oz) of white meat per serve.
- Recipes for offal or 'variety meats', such as liver, kidney, tongue, brains, tripe and sweetbreads, have not been included in this book, because of their high saturated fat or cholesterol content. In some circumstances offal may be included in the diet because of its nutritional value; however, the cholesterol content should be kept in mind.
- Pork, ham and bacon are also in the high cholesterol category, and we suggest that these meats be reserved for special occasions.

Sauerbraten ingredients (page 122)

BEEF

Beef Bundaberg

Serves: 4
Cooking time: 10 minutes

840 kJ (200 cal) per serve

4 fillet steaks, about 125 g (4 oz) each
3 tablespoons tomato paste
4 tablespoons dry sherry
¼ teaspoon monosodium glutamate
1 clove garlic, crushed

2 teaspoons Worcestershire sauce
4-6 drops Tabasco sauce
4 spring onions or shallots, chopped
salt
black pepper, freshly ground

1 Trim any visible fat from steaks.
2 Mix all other ingredients together, and marinate steaks in this mixture for 4 hours, turning occasionally.
3 Preheat griller and grill steaks for 5 minutes on each side for medium-rare, or longer if desired. Baste with the marinade to prevent drying, while cooking.

Stuffed Peppers

Serves: 4
Cooking time: 1 hour
Oven temperature: 180°C (350°F)

750 kJ (180 cal) per serve

4 large green peppers (capsicums)
250 g (8 oz) lean topside, finely minced
2 beef stock cubes, crumbled
2 stalks celery, finely chopped
1 medium carrot, peeled and grated
1 medium onion, finely chopped

1 medium tomato, finely chopped
125 g (4 oz) mushrooms, peeled and finely chopped
pinch mixed dried herbs
salt
2 tablespoons tomato paste

Garnish
4 slices tomato
4 sprigs parsley

1 Preheat oven to 180°C (350°F).
2 Remove tops from peppers, cut out seeds and pith.
3 Combine remaining ingredients.
4 Spoon filling into shells.
5 Bake at 180°C (350°F) for 1 hour.
6 Serve garnished with tomato and parsley.

Steak Dianne

Serves: 6　　　　　　　　　　　　　　　　　　*920 kJ (220 cal) per serve*
Cooking time: 10 minutes

**750 g (1½ lb) rump steak, cut
  thinly**
salt
black pepper, freshly ground

1 tablespoon polyunsaturated oil
2 tablespoons finely chopped fresh parsley
2 cloves garlic, crushed
1 tablespoon Worcestershire sauce

1 Remove visible fat from steak and cut steak into 4 even pieces.
2 Rub each piece with salt and pepper.
3 Heat oil in a flat pan.
4 Fry meat on each side for 1 minute.
5 Sprinkle with parsley and garlic and cook for 7 minutes.
6 Add Worcestershire sauce, toss meat over heat for another minute and serve.

Drunken Beef

Serves: 4　　　　　　　　　　　　　　　　　　*905 kJ (215 cal) per serve*
Cooking time: 10 minutes

500 g (1 lb) fillet or rump steak
**1½ cups canned champignons, drained
  and sliced**
6 spring onions or shallots

¼ cup whisky
salt
2 tablespoons non-fat natural yoghurt

Garnish
paprika

1 Trim visible fat from meat and cut meat into 2.5 cm (1 in) pieces.
2 Dry-fry meat in a pan. Meat should be well browned.
3 Add champignons, onions and whisky, and cook for 1-2 minutes or until the whisky has almost evaporated.
4 Remove from heat, stir in the yoghurt (beaten well to remove any lumps).
5 Serve, sprinkled with paprika.

Apple-Stuffed Steaks

Serves: 4　　　　　　　　　　　　　　　　　　*845 kJ (200 cal) per serve*
Cooking time: 10 minutes

4 fillet steaks, about 125 g (4 oz) each
1 tablespoon chopped fresh parsley
1 apple, peeled and grated

1 spring onion or shallot, sliced finely
1 teaspoon chopped fresh sage
salt

1 Trim visible fat from meat. Cut a pocket in the side of each steak.
2 Mix remaining ingredients together. Stuff one-quarter of the mixture into each steak, and close the pocket with a toothpick or thread.
3 Grill for approximately 5 minutes on each side for medium rare or longer if desired. Remove toothpick or thread and serve.

Baked Corned Silverside

Serves: 6
Cooking time: 2 hours
Oven temperature: 180°C (350°F)

815 kJ (190 cal) per serve

750 g (1½ lb) corned silverside	½ teaspoon hot dry mustard
1 medium onion	1 teaspoon ground cinnamon
2 medium carrots	juice of 1 orange
2 stalks celery	1 teaspoon soy sauce
6 cloves	

1 Rinse meat, remove visible fat and place in a saucepan and cover with water.
2 Roughly cut onion, carrots and celery and add to the saucepan.
3 Bring to the boil and simmer for 1 hour.
4 Cool in the liquid and then drain meat, discard vegetables.
5 Press cloves into meat, leaving about 5 cm (2 in) between cloves.
6 Place meat in an oven bag and into a roasting dish.
7 Mix the mustard, cinnamon, orange juice and soy sauce and pour into the oven bag over meat, covering well.
8 Seal oven bag and bake meat in the oven for 1 hour at 180°C (350°F), turning at intervals.
9 Remove cloves from meat and serve sliced, hot or cold.

Sauerbraten

Serves: 8
Cooking time: 2-2½ hours

780 kJ (185 cal) per serve

1 kg (2 lb) top round or buttock of beef	1 stalk celery, chopped
1½ cups dry red wine	½ lemon, sliced
½ cup wine vinegar	2 bay leaves
2 teaspoons salt	6 cloves
½ teaspoon black pepper, freshly ground	6 allspice or juniper berries
1 medium onion, sliced	6 sprigs parsley
1 medium carrot, sliced	

1 Remove visible fat from meat, roll and tie and place into a deep bowl.
2 Combine the wine, vinegar, salt, pepper, onion, carrot, celery, lemon, bay leaves, cloves, allspice or juniper berries and parsley in a saucepan.
3 Bring to the boil and pour over meat.
4 Cover bowl and refrigerate for 3 days, turning meat twice daily.
5 Remove meat and heat marinade in a large saucepan.
6 Plunge meat into boiling marinade and seal on both sides.
7 Reduce the heat and simmer gently for 2-2½ hours.
8 Skim fat from liquid and strain broth.
9 Slice meat and serve with a spoonful of broth poured over meat.

Rabbit Bouillabaisse (page 115)

Pocket Beef

Serves: 6   *855 kJ (205 cal) per serve*
Cooking time: 1¼ hours
Oven temperature: 190°C (375°F)

750 g (1½ lb) corner topside   **salt and pepper**
1 stalk celery   **pinch mixed dried herbs**
1 carrot

1 Trim visible fat from meat. With a sharp knife cut about 10 small, evenly spaced pockets from the front to the back of the meat.
2 Cut celery and carrot into slices as long as the pockets are deep and about 1 cm x 1 cm (½ in x ½ in) in width and thickness.
3 Toss celery and carrot in salt, pepper and herbs and push into pockets using celery and carrot alternately.
4 Place into an oven bag, tie and bake for 1¼ hours at 190°C (375°F).
5 Serve sliced, either hot or cold.

Roast Beef and Apricots

Serves: 6   *920 kJ (220 cal) per serve*
Cooking time: 1½ hours
Oven temperature: 190°C (375°F)

1 kg (2 lb) corner topside   **2 cups canned unsweetened drained**
salt and pepper   **   apricot halves**
                                          ½ cup water

1 Trim visible fat from meat. Rub meat with salt and pepper, and place in an oven bag.
2 Purée 1 cup apricots with ½ cup water.
3 Pour into bag, secure. Bake for 1½ hours.
4 Ten minutes before serving, place remaining apricot halves in oven to heat.
5 Slice and serve meat with juice and apricot halves.

Swiss Steak

Serves: 6   *865 kJ (205 cal) per serve*
Cooking time: 1½-2 hours

750 g (1½ lb) rump or blade steak   **2 cups peeled canned tomatoes**
salt   **1 medium white onion, finely diced**
black pepper, freshly ground

1 Remove visible fat from meat and cut meat into serving-size pieces.
2 Season with salt and pepper.
3 Place tomatoes with juice into a flat pan or flameproof casserole and bring to the boil.
4 Add meat to boiling tomato liquid.
5 Add onion, reduce heat, cover pan and cook very slowly for 1½-2 hours.

Steak au Poivre

Serves: 6
Cooking time: approx. 10 minutes

830 kJ (200 cal) per serve

750 g (1½ lb) rump steak
1 tablespoon whole black peppercorns, crushed
salt
1 tablespoon skim milk powder

½ cup water
½ teaspoon polyunsaturated oil
1 tablespoon brandy
½ teaspoon Worcestershire sauce
1 teaspoon lemon juice

1　Remove visible fat from meat and cut meat into 4 even pieces.
2　Press pepper and salt into all sides of steak.
3　Combine skim milk powder with water, set aside.
4　Rub a large frying pan with oil, and heat.
5　Seal the steak quickly for 30 seconds on both sides and then cook for a further 3 minutes on both sides.
6　Pour brandy over meat, heat and ignite.
7　When flame dies down, remove steak from pan and place onto serving plates.
8　Pour Worcestershire sauce, lemon juice and skim milk into the pan. Stir well over the heat.
9　Pour sauce over steaks and serve.

Fillet with Mushrooms

Serves: 4
Cooking time: 10 minutes

965 kJ (230 cal) per serve

4 fillet steaks, about 125 g (4 oz) each
salt
black pepper, freshly ground
2 teaspoons polyunsaturated oil
4 tablespoons water

125 g (4 oz) fresh button mushrooms, stems removed
1 medium white onion, finely chopped
2 tablespoons non-fat natural yoghurt

Garnish
1 teaspoon finely chopped fresh parsley

1　Remove visible fat from meat and shape meat into round pieces and tie to ensure meat retains shape during cooking.
2　Season with salt and pepper.
3　Heat oil in a pan and sauté meat until well browned (3 minutes on each side for medium rare, or longer if desired). Remove meat and place in the oven to keep warm.
4　Add water to pan and stir in remaining meat juices. Add mushrooms and onion, cover and cook for 4 minutes.
5　Place yoghurt into a bowl and slowly add juices from the pan to make a creamy sauce.
6　Mix mushrooms and onions into the sauce, pour over steaks immediately and serve sprinkled with parsley.

Argentina Meat Roll

Serves: 8
Cooking time: 1½ hours
Oven temperature: 180°C (350°F)

940 kJ (225 cal) per serve

1 kg (2 lb) thin skirt steak (in one piece)
salt and pepper
1 medium carrot, peeled and cut into
 thin slivers

6 spring onions or shallots, sliced
 lengthwise into slivers
125 g (4 oz) fresh green beans, topped,
 tailed and sliced in half lengthwise

Sauce
2 tablespoons red wine vinegar
½ teaspoon dry mustard
1 beef stock cube, crumbled

pinch mixed dried herbs
salt

Basting mixture
1 tablespoon polyunsaturated oil
black pepper
½ teaspoon monosodium glutamate

1 Preheat oven to 180°C (350°F).
2 Flatten meat with a meat mallet to form a rectangle about 20 cm (8 in) x 40 cm (16 in). Sprinkle with salt and pepper.
3 Place vegetables across meat.
4 Mix sauce ingredients together, spoon over vegetables.
5 Roll meat and tie securely in several places to hold the roll.
6 Place in a baking dish. Rub basting mixture over meat.
7 Bake for 1½ hours at 180°C (350°F). Remove meat and allow to cool for 10 minutes. Baste occasionally with any juices. Remove string, slice and serve.

Beef Shin Bake

Serves: 4
Cooking time: 2 hours
Oven temperature: 190°C (375°F)

1005 kJ (240 cal) per serve

4 slices of beef shin
1 cup peeled canned tomatoes
½ cup water
1 medium carrot, diced
1 medium onion, sliced

125 g (4 oz) fresh button mushrooms
2 slices fresh pineapple, diced, or ½ cup
 drained canned pineapple pieces
salt and pepper
pinch mixed dried herbs

1 Remove visible fat from shins and place shins in a casserole dish.
2 Pour tomatoes and water over the shins.
3 Sprinkle with carrot, onion, mushrooms, pineapple, salt, pepper and herbs.
4 Cover and bake in the oven at 190°C (375°F) for 1¾ hours or until meat is tender.
5 Uncover and bake for a further 15 minutes.
Note: This dish is best prepared on the previous day. Refrigerate, and remove fat before reheating.

Steak and Mushroom Casserole

Serves: 6   *980 kJ (235 cal) per serve*
Cooking time: 1¼ hours

750 g (1½ lb) rump steak
2 teaspoons polyunsaturated oil
12-16 baby onions
250 g (8 oz) fresh mushrooms, peeled
  and sliced
1 cup claret

2 beef stock cubes
pinch mixed dried herbs
1 bay leaf
2 tablespoons tomato paste
salt and pepper

1 Trim all visible fat from meat and cut meat into 2.5 cm (1 in) pieces.
2 Fry meat in oil until browned on all sides. Remove from the pan and place in a heavy saucepan.
3 Add onions and mushrooms to pan and brown. Remove and add to meat.
4 Pour wine into pan to dissolve brownings. Add stock cubes, herbs, bay leaf, tomato paste, salt and pepper. Stir until well mixed.
5 Pour over meat and vegetables.
6 Simmer gently with lid on for one hour.
7 If cooking liquid is thin, remove lid during the last 10 minutes prior to serving.

Beef Olives

Serves: 6   *890 kJ (215 cal) per serve*
Cooking time: 1½-1¾ hours
Oven temperature: 190°C (375°F)

Filling

1 large onion, finely chopped
375 g (12 oz) fresh mushrooms,
  finely chopped
salt and pepper

pinch dried oregano
2 teaspoons finely chopped fresh parsley
2 tablespoons water

Beef olives

12 thin, oblong slices of topside, each
  weighing 60-90 g (2-3 oz)
salt and pepper

pinch mixed dried herbs
3 tablespoons tomato paste
1 cup water

1 Place filling ingredients in a saucepan and simmer for 10 minutes or until soft.
2 Remove visible fat from meat and spread each slice with filling.
3 Roll each piece of meat and fasten with small toothpicks.
4 Place in a flat casserole dish and sprinkle with salt, pepper and herbs.
5 Mix tomato paste with water and pour over the beef olives.
6 Cover and bake in the oven at 190°C (375°F) for 1¼-1½ hours.
7 Remove toothpicks and serve hot.

Country Casserole

Serves: 4
Cooking time: 1½ hours

1120 kJ (265 cal) per serve

500 g (1 lb) topside steak
2 teaspoons polyunsaturated oil
250 g (8 oz) fresh baby carrots, peeled
2 stalks celery, chopped roughly
1 large onion, chopped roughly
1 medium tomato, chopped roughly
1 medium green pepper (capsicum),
  chopped roughly

½ cup dry red wine
½ cup water
2 beef stock cubes
salt
2 tablespoons tomato paste

Garnish
parsley, chopped

1 Trim visible fat from meat. Cut meat into 2.5 cm (1 in) pieces.
2 Heat oil in heavy saucepan, add beef and brown. Remove meat and set aside. Add vegetables to pan and brown well.
3 Return meat to pan.
4 Add wine, water, stock cubes and salt. Bring liquid to the boil, reduce heat and simmer covered for 1 hour.
5 Remove lid, simmer for a further 15 minutes to reduce cooking liquid. Stir in tomato paste.
6 Serve, garnished with parsley.

Bombay Beef

Serves: 4
Cooking time: 1½ hours

1085 kJ (260 cal) per serve

500 g (1 lb) blade steak
1 medium carrot
1 medium onion
1 stalk celery
1 tablespoon curry powder

1 cup water
salt and pepper
250 g (8 oz) tomatoes, peeled and diced
1 medium apple, diced
1 medium banana, diced

1 Remove visible fat from meat and cut meat into 2.5 cm (1 in) cubes.
2 Dice the carrot, onion and celery.
3 Heat the curry powder in a dry saucepan for 30 seconds, then add water, meat, carrot, onion, celery, salt and pepper.
4 Simmer covered for 1¼ hours or until meat is tender, add tomatoes.
5 Remove lid and simmer for a further 10 minutes.
6 Add apple and banana to the saucepan and simmer for 5 minutes. Serve.

Hungarian Goulash

Serves: 4
Cooking time: 1 hour 15 minutes

905 kJ (215 cal) per serve

500 g (1 lb) topside or rump steak
3 teaspoons paprika
2 medium onions, sliced
3 tablespoons tomato paste

salt
black pepper
½ cup water

Garnish
2 tablespoons non-fat natural yoghurt
parsley, chopped

1 Trim visible fat from meat and cut meat into 2.5 cm (1 in) pieces.
2 Dry-fry meat and paprika until meat is well browned.
3 Add onions and cook until soft.
4 Stir in tomato paste, salt, pepper and water.
5 Cover and cook slowly for one hour or until meat is tender. Check flavour and add more salt if necessary.
6 Serve, garnished with yoghurt (which has been stirred well to remove any lumps), and parsley.

Beef Stroganoff

Serves: 6
Cooking time: 10 minutes

890 kJ (215 cal) per serve

750 g (1½ lb) rump or fillet of beef
black pepper, freshly ground
salt
½ cup water
¼ cup unsweetened tomato juice

1 tablespoon brandy
250 g (½ lb) fresh button mushrooms
8 spring onions or shallots, sliced
¼ cup non-fat natural yoghurt

1 Remove visible fat from meat and cut meat across the grain into slices 1 cm (½ in) thick.
2 Season to taste with pepper and salt, and flatten each slice with a meat mallet.
3 Place water and tomato juice into a large frying pan and bring to the boil.
4 Add meat and cook quickly for 5 minutes.
5 Drain off liquid from pan and retain.
6 Pour brandy over meat, heat and ignite.
7 When flame dies, pour juices back into the pan.
8 Add mushrooms and cook for 4 minutes.
9 Stir in spring onions.
10 Remove from heat and add yoghurt. Serve.

Meatball and Apricot Skewers

Serves: 4
Cooking time: 10 minutes

1085 kJ (260 cal) per serve

Meatballs

500 g (1 lb) lean topside, finely minced
1 medium onion, chopped finely
2 teaspoons chopped fresh mint
3 tablespoons chopped fresh parsley
2 beef stock cubes, crumbled
salt

½ teaspoon monosodium glutamate
1 teaspoon Worcestershire sauce
1 egg white
pinch mixed dried herbs
2 cups drained unsweetened apricot halves

Marinade

½ cup unsweetened pineapple juice
1 tablespoon soy sauce

1 x 2.5 cm (1 in) piece green ginger, sliced finely

1 Mix meatball ingredients together well. Divide into 4.
2 Shape each quantity of mixture into 6 meatballs.
3 Thread 3 meatballs on each skewer alternately with apricot halves.
4 Place on a tray or shallow dish.
5 Pour marinade over. Marinate for one hour, turning occasionally.
6 Place skewers under a hot griller or on a barbecue and cook for 5 minutes, then turn and cook for a further 5 minutes, basting with marinade frequently.
7 Serve immediately. Allow 2 skewers per person.

Beef in Wine Sauce

Serves: 6
Cooking time: 45 minutes

970 kJ (230 cal) per serve

750 g (1½ lb) rump steak
1 tablespoon polyunsaturated oil
2 medium onions, chopped
2 cloves garlic, crushed
2 beef stock cubes, crumbled

1 cup claret
2 tablespoons tomato paste
1 bay leaf
pinch dried thyme
salt and pepper

Garnish
chopped parsley

1 Trim visible fat from meat. Cut meat into 2.5 cm (1 in) cubes.
2 Heat oil, add meat and brown. Lift meat out and place in a saucepan.
3 Add onions and garlic to the pan, fry until soft, then add to meat. Drain any oil from pan.
4 Add stock cubes and claret to the pan and dissolve any brownings.
5 Add tomato paste, herbs, salt and pepper. Check flavour. Bring to the boil.
6 Pour sauce over meat. Simmer very gently in a covered saucepan for 40 minutes.
7 Serve, garnished with chopped parsley.

Korean Barbecue Beef

Serves: 4   *1170 kJ (205 cal) per serve*

500 g (1 lb) rump steak
1 cup soy sauce
2 teaspoons finely chopped green ginger
2 teaspoons brandy
8 spring onions or shallots

185 g (6 oz) silverbeet or spinach,
  finely shredded
185 g (6 oz) fresh mushrooms, finely sliced
185 g (6 oz) bean shoots
6 cups Basic Meat Stock (see page 45)

1   Remove all visible fat from meat and finely slice meat across the grain into wafer-thin pieces approximately 5 cm (2 in) square.
2   Marinate meat in ½ cup soy sauce, 1 teaspoon green ginger, and 2 teaspoons brandy for 1 hour.
3   Slice the spring onions lengthways and cut into pieces approximately 5 cm (2 in) long.
4   Arrange silverbeet or spinach, mushrooms, spring onions, bean shoots and meat on a flat platter.
5   Mix the remaining soy sauce and ginger and place in a small dish.
6   The beef should be cooked at the table in a steam boat or fondue pot. To serve, heat the stock, pour into the steam boat or fondue pot and place over a flame on the table.
7   Place platter containing meat and vegetables and the dish of soy sauce and ginger on the table.
8   Each guest should be given a small bowl, chopsticks and a spoon, or a spoon and fork.
9   Guests select pieces of meat and vegetables and drop these into the hot stock to cook quickly for 1-2 minutes.
10 The soy sauce and ginger may be sprinkled over the food when it is cooked.

Note: The flavour of the stock becomes richer during cooking and can be served as a soup during the meal. If necessary, more water may be added to the stock at intervals.

Tropical Burgers

Serves: 4   *1005 kJ (240 cal) per serve*
Cooking time: 25-30 minutes

500 g (1 lb) lean topside, finely minced
salt and pepper
pinch mixed dried herbs

2 cups unsweetened canned pineapple,
  drained and juice reserved
6 spring onions or shallots, chopped

1   Mix meat with salt, pepper and herbs.
2   Shape into 8 even, round pieces and place in a large frying pan.
3   Pour juice over meat.
4   Cover and simmer for 20 minutes.
5   Add pineapple to frying pan and simmer for a further 5 minutes.
6   Add spring onions, cook for 2 minutes and serve.

Chop Suey

Serves: 4   *1085 kJ (260 cal) per serve*
Cooking time: 15 minutes

500 g (1 lb) rump steak, fat removed,
  finely sliced
1 teaspoon polyunsaturated oil
1 medium onion, chopped
1 stalk celery, chopped
125 g (4 oz) French beans, cut into
  2.5 cm (1 in) strips

1 small green pepper (capsicum), chopped
1 small red pepper (capsicum), chopped
2 cups chopped cabbage
3 tablespoons soy sauce
½ teaspoon monosodium glutamate

1 Dry-fry meat until brown, draining any juice and fat as it appears. Remove meat and place in the oven to keep hot.
2 Add oil to the pan and fry all vegetables except cabbage until just cooked and still crisp. Set aside with meat.
3 Add cabbage, soy sauce and monosodium glutamate to the pan and cook for 3 minutes.
4 Return meat and vegetables to the pan. Heat through, stirring until well mixed. Serve immediately.

Sliced Beef and Broccoli

Serves: 4   *1350 kJ (320 cal) per serve*
Cooking time: 15 minutes

500 g (1 lb) lean rump steak
3 cloves garlic, crushed
4 tablespoons dry sherry
4 tablespoons soy sauce
1 tablespoon thinly sliced green ginger

¼ teaspoon monosodium glutamate
2 tablespoons polyunsaturated oil
1 small bunch broccoli, thick stalks
  discarded

1 Slice beef thinly into strips.
2 Mix garlic, sherry, soy sauce, ginger and monosodium glutamate together in a bowl.
3 Add meat, mix well, and marinate for 2 hours.
4 Heat 1 tablespoon of oil in a wok or large frying pan.
5 Add broccoli, cover and cook for 5 minutes.
6 Remove broccoli and keep hot.
7 Add the remainder of oil, turn heat high, add meat and cook rapidly until all juices have evaporated and meat starts to brown.
8 Add broccoli and stir until heated through.
9 Serve immediately.

Stuffed Marrow

Serves: 4   *760 kJ (180 cal) per serve*
Cooking time: 1¾-2 hours
Oven temperature: 190°C (375°F)

375 g (12 oz) lean topside, finely minced
1 medium onion, chopped
1 small carrot, grated
½ cup water
salt and pepper

pinch mixed dried herbs
3 tablespoons tomato paste
1 tablespoon soy sauce
1 small marrow, approximately 1 kg (2 lb)

1   Place all ingredients except marrow into a saucepan, mix well and simmer for 20 minutes.
2   Halve marrow lengthways and scrape out all seeds.
3   Heap filling into one half of marrow and top with the other half.
4   Score skin on top of marrow, marking into 8 even slices.
5   Tie the two halves together and place on a flat baking dish.
6   Bake in the oven for 1½-1¾ hours at 190°C (375°F).
7   Remove ties and slice into sections.
8   Serve two slices per person.

Steak and Black Bean Sauce

Serves: 4   *1265 kJ (300 cal) per serve*
Cooking time: 8 minutes

500 g (1 lb) fillet steak
1 tablespoon polyunsaturated oil
2 teaspoons brandy
1 tablespoon soy sauce
½ clove garlic, crushed
½ teaspoon finely chopped green ginger

salt
¼ teaspoon monosodium glutamate
2 tablespoons black beans
½ cup diced green pepper (capsicum)
½ cup diced red pepper (capsicum)
¼ cup water

Garnish
6 spring onions or shallots, chopped

1   Remove visible fat from steak and cut steak across the grain into wafer-thin slices.
2   Mix steak with oil, 1 teaspoon brandy, soy sauce, garlic, ginger, salt and monosodium glutamate.
3   Marinate for 15 minutes.
4   Pour sufficient boiling water over black beans to cover, stand for 10 minutes, then drain.
5   Add the remaining brandy to the beans and mash with a fork.
6   Heat a wok or frying pan.
7   Dry-fry meat lightly, stirring constantly, until just sealed. Remove and keep warm.
8   Add peppers to the pan and stir over heat for 3 minutes. Remove and keep warm.
9   Add beans and stir over a high heat for 1 minute.
10 Return meat, peppers and juices to the pan with ¼ cup water.
11 Bring to the boil, simmer for 1 minute.
12 Garnish with spring onions and serve.

Savoury Cabbage Rolls

Serves: 4
Cooking time: 1 hour
Oven temperature: 190°C (375°F)

900 kJ (215 cal) per serve

Filling

375 g (12 oz) lean topside, finely minced
1 medium onion, chopped
1 small carrot, grated
½ cup water

salt and pepper
pinch mixed dried herbs
3 tablespoons tomato paste
1 tablespoon soy sauce

Cabbage rolls

8 large cabbage leaves, whole
1 cup tomato juice

1 Place all ingredients for filling into a saucepan, mix well and simmer for 20 minutes.
2 Drain sauce from pan and set aside.
3 Remove fat from top of sauce with kitchen paper.
4 Place cabbage leaves in boiling, salted water and simmer for 5 minutes.
5 Drain cabbage leaves and lie each leaf flat.
6 Place equal quantities of meat on each leaf.
7 Roll cabbage leaves around the meat filling, folding in edges of leaves.
8 Place cabbage rolls in a flat casserole dish, and pour over tomato juice and meat juices.
9 Cover and bake in the oven for 25 minutes at 190°C (375°F).
10 Uncover and bake for a further 15 minutes.
11 Serve hot, allowing 2 rolls per person.

Mexican Chilli

Serves: 4
Cooking time: 1½ hours

1150 kJ (275 cal) per serve

2 medium onions, chopped
2 teaspoons polyunsaturated oil
500 g (1 lb) lean topside, finely minced
4 garlic cloves, crushed
2 beef stock cubes
500 g (1 lb) tomatoes, chopped
1 cup water

½ cup tomato paste
salt
1 bay leaf
pinch dried dill
1 teaspoon chilli powder
10 drops Tabasco sauce

Accompaniment
Tossed Salad (see page 52)

1 Fry onions in hot oil. Add beef, fry until brown and skim off any excess fat.
2 Add garlic, beef cubes, tomatoes and water. Simmer 15 minutes.
3 Add tomato paste, salt, herbs, chilli powder and Tabasco sauce.
4 Transfer mixture to a heavy saucepan and simmer covered for 1 hour, stirring occasionally.
5 If mixture is too liquid, leave lid off for the last 10 minutes of cooking time.
6 Serve in bowls, accompanied by Tossed Salad.

Chinese Steak and Vegetables

Serves: 6
Cooking time: 12 minutes

880 kJ (210 cal) per serve

750 g (1½ lb) rump steak
salt
2 tablespoons soy sauce
6 spring onions or shallots

1 beef stock cube
1 cup water
125 g (4 oz) mushrooms, sliced
125 g (4 oz) bean shoots

1   Remove visible fat from meat and slice meat across the grain into strips 50 mm x 5 mm x 5 mm (2 in x ¼ in x ¼ in).
2   Mix meat with salt and soy sauce, and marinate for 30 minutes.
3   Chop spring onions into 1 cm (½ in) pieces, separating the white sections from the green.
4   Dissolve stock cube in boiling water and pour into a wok or large frying pan.
5   Bring to the boil, drop meat into the boiling liquid. Simmer for 5 minutes.
6   Remove meat from pan, add mushrooms, cook for 3-4 minutes and remove.
7   Return liquid to the boil, add bean shoots and white sections of spring onions and cook for 2 minutes.
8   Add meat, mushrooms and green sections of spring onions. Stir, reheat and serve.

Sweet and Sour Meatballs

Serves: 4
Cooking time: 30 minutes

1085 kJ (260 cal) per serve

Sauce

1 medium white onion
1 small carrot
1 small green pepper (capsicum)
1 stalk celery
salt

½ teaspoon finely chopped green ginger
1 clove garlic, finely chopped
1½ cups unsweetened tomato juice
1 cup unsweetened pineapple pieces, juice included

Meatballs

500 g (1 lb) lean topside, finely minced
1 small onion, finely chopped
pinch mixed dried herbs

salt
1 egg white

1   Cut the onion, carrot, green pepper (capsicum) and celery into fine strips, each about the shape and size of a matchstick.
2   Place all the sauce ingredients in a saucepan, and bring to the boil.
3   Combine meatball ingredients.
4   Roll mixture into small balls (quantity should make 20 balls).
5   Drop meatballs into sauce and simmer for ½ hour.

Lamb Shanks Jardinière (page 151)

Taraba

Serves: 4   *1120 kJ (265 cal) per serve*
Cooking time: 30 minutes

Meatballs

1 bunch silverbeet or spinach
500 g (1 lb) lean topside, finely minced
4 cloves garlic, crushed
1 small onion, finely chopped
salt

1 beef stock cube, crumbled
juice of ½ lemon
pinch dried rosemary
pinch dried marjoram
1 egg white

Sauce

2 cups tomato purée
pinch dried oregano

¼ teaspoon garlic salt
black pepper

1 Wash silverbeet or spinach, drain and remove stalks. Cut each leaf into half.
2 Mix meatball ingredients together.
3 Place 2 tablespoons of meat mixture on each silverbeet or spinach leaf and wrap well.
4 Place meatballs in a large saucepan, packing tightly.
5 Mix sauce ingredients together and pour over meatballs.
6 Simmer gently for 30 minutes or until cooked.
7 Remove meatballs to heated serving dish. Keep hot.
8 Reduce sauce by boiling rapidly until fairly thick.
9 Pour over meatballs and serve.

Apricot Meat Loaf

Serves: 8   *955 kJ (230 cal) per serve*
Cooking time: 1 hour
Oven temperature: 180°C (350°F)

Meat loaf

1 kg (2 lb) lean topside, finely minced
2 beef stock cubes, crumbled
1 medium onion, finely chopped
salt and pepper
pinch mixed dried herbs

2 egg whites
4 tablespoons tomato paste
pinch dry mustard
½ cup artificially sweetened apricot
** halves, drained, and juice reserved**

Sauce

1 cup syrup from apricots
½ cup artificially sweetened apricot
** halves, drained and chopped**

6 tablespoons tomato paste
1 teaspoon dry mustard

1 Mix meat loaf ingredients thoroughly.
2 Shape into a loaf and place in a baking dish or loaf pan.
3 Combine sauce ingredients and pour over meat loaf. Bake for 1 hour at 180°C (350°F).
4 Place on heated platter to serve.

Cottage Loaf

Serves: 4
Cooking time: 1 hour
Oven temperature: 190°C (375°F)

895 kJ (210 cal) per serve

500 g (1 lb) lean topside, finely minced
salt and pepper
pinch mixed dried herbs
1 egg white

1 small carrot, grated
1 medium tomato, diced
1 medium onion, diced

1 Combine all ingredients.
2 Place a strip of aluminium foil onto the bottom of a flat baking dish.
3 Tip meat mixture onto foil and shape into a loaf, or use a loaf tin.
4 Place in the oven and bake for 1 hour at 190°C (375°F).
5 Serve sliced, hot or cold.

LAMB

Launceston Lamb

Serves: 4
Cooking time: 1½ hours

955 kJ (230 cal) per serve

500 g (1 lb) leg lamb, boned
2 cups peeled tomatoes
salt and pepper
½ teaspoon finely chopped fresh
  rosemary

2 tablespoons dry sherry
¼ cup water
2 cooking apples, peeled and diced

1 Trim all visible fat and gristle from meat. Cut meat into 2.5 cm (1 in) cubes.
2 Drain juice from tomatoes into a saucepan.
3 Add meat, salt, pepper, rosemary, sherry and water.
4 Bring to the boil, lower heat and simmer for 1¼ hours, stirring occasionally.
5 Gently stir in tomatoes and apples. Cook for 15 minutes and serve.

Navarin of Lamb

Serves: 4
Cooking time: 1 hour 15 minutes

1240 kJ (295 cal) per serve

500 g (1 lb) lean leg lamb, boned
1 tablespoon polyunsaturated oil
1 stalk celery, roughly chopped
1 medium carrot, roughly chopped
125 g (4 oz) potatoes, peeled and
  roughly chopped
1 large onion, roughly chopped
1 large tomato, roughly chopped
½ cup dry sherry

½ cup water
2 beef stock cubes
4 tablespoons tomato paste
salt and pepper
1 tablespoon chopped fresh mint
1 teaspoon chopped fresh sage
2 cloves garlic, crushed
60 g (2 oz) green peas

Garnish
parsley, chopped

1 Cut meat into 5 cm (2 in) pieces and add to heated oil in a frying pan. Add vegetables and lightly brown.
2 Remove meat and vegetables, and drain oil from the pan. Add sherry, water, stock cubes, tomato paste, salt and pepper. Simmer gently for 5 minutes, dissolving brownings. Return meat and vegetables to the pan. Add herbs and garlic.
3 Cover and simmer gently for 45 minutes. Add peas and cook for a further 10 minutes.
4 Serve, garnished with parsley.

Navarin of Lamb

Lemon Lamb Shanks

Serves: 4
Cooking time: 1¾ hours
Oven temperature: 200°C (400°F)

655 kJ (155 cal) per serve

4 lamb shanks
juice of 3 lemons
6 garlic cloves, crushed

3 tablespoons soy sauce
salt and pepper

Garnish
parsley sprigs

1 Trim all visible fat from meat.
2 Dry-fry shanks in a frying pan to brown meat.
3 Place in a baking dish, add lemon juice, garlic, soy sauce, salt and pepper.
4 Bake in the oven for ½ hour at 200°C (400°F), reduce oven temperature to 180°C (350°F) and cook for a further hour.
5 Serve with parsley garnish.

Moussaka

Serves: 6
Cooking time: 30-35 minutes
Oven temperature: 190°C (375°F)

1350 kJ (320 cal) per serve

750 g (1½ lb) lean leg lamb, finely minced
1 beef stock cube
1 cup water
1 large onion, finely chopped
2 cloves garlic, finely chopped
250 g (8 oz) mushrooms, sliced
500 g (1 lb) tomatoes, peeled, seeded and chopped

2 tablespoons finely chopped fresh parsley
2 tablespoons tomato paste
salt
black pepper
1.5 kg (3 lb) aubergine (eggplant)
300 g (10 oz) non-fat cottage cheese

1 Place minced lamb, stock cube and water in a saucepan and bring to the boil.
2 Add onion, garlic, mushrooms, tomatoes, parsley, tomato paste, salt and pepper. Simmer for 20 minutes.
3 Slice unpeeled aubergine lengthwise into thin slices, place in a pan with a small quantity of boiling salted water, cover with lid and cook for 2 minutes. Drain.
4 Line a baking dish with slices of aubergine, cover with meat mixture, spread with cottage cheese and top with a further layer of aubergine.
5 Continue this layering until baking dish is full, finishing with a layer of aubergine.
6 Spread with remaining cottage cheese and bake in an oven at 190°C (375°F) for approximately 10 minutes or until the top begins to brown.

Note: The meat mixture is best prepared and cooked the day before use, and the fat removed.

Kibby

Serves: 4
Cooking time: 20 minutes

855 kJ (205 cal) per serve

Meat

500 g (1 lb) lean leg lamb, boned and finely minced

1 egg white

salt and pepper

1 tablespoon wheatgerm

Stuffing

1 small onion, minced

2 teaspoons chopped fresh mint

1 teaspoon chopped fresh parsley

¼ teaspoon paprika

salt and pepper

1 Combine minced lamb with egg white, salt, pepper and wheatgerm.
2 Mix stuffing ingredients together.
3 Shape meat mixture into rolls. Make a hollow in the centre of each, stuff, and close the end.
4 Cook under a hot griller, turning frequently to ensure even browning.
5 When serving, allow 3 meat rolls per person.

Lamb Saté

Serves: 4
Cooking time: 5 minutes

1060 kJ (255 cal) per serve

500 g (1 lb) leg lamb, boned

1 clove garlic, crushed

3 tablespoons soy sauce

2 tablespoons lemon juice

pinch chilli powder

1 small onion, grated

salt

1 teaspoon polyunsaturated oil

2 cups drained unsweetened apricots

1 Trim visible fat from meat, and cut meat into 1 cm (½ in) cubes.
2 Thread onto skewers (approximately 5 cubes per skewer).
3 Combine remaining ingredients except apricots, and place lamb in marinade for at least 2 hours, turning at intervals.
4 Grill over a hot coal fire or under a griller, turning frequently and basting with the marinade.
5 Purée apricots in an electric blender or by passing through a wire sieve.
6 Add marinade, bring to the boil and serve with hot lamb saté.

Somerset Steamed Lamb

Serves: 8
Cooking time: 2½-3 hours

735 kJ (175 cal) per serve

1½ kg (3 lb) leg of lamb

3 tablespoons finely chopped fresh mint

2 tablespoons coarsely ground salt

black pepper, freshly ground

1 Remove all visible fat from lamb.
2 Place leg of lamb on a clean cloth. Rub entire surface of lamb with mint, salt and pepper.
3 Wrap meat firmly in cloth and place in the top section of a large double steamer. Fill the bottom section three-quarters full of boiling water.
4 Cover the steamer, and cook lamb for 2½-3 hours.
5 Serve hot or cold, allowing 125 g (4 oz) per serve.

Moroccan Kefta

Serves: 4
Cooking time: 1¼-1½ hours

900 kJ (215 cal) per serve

Meatballs

500 g (1 lb) lean leg lamb, boned and finely minced
1 small white onion, finely chopped
¼ teaspoon finely chopped fresh mint
1 teaspoon finely chopped fresh parsley
¼ teaspoon dried marjoram

salt
black pepper, freshly ground
1 pinch each of ground cumin, cayenne pepper, paprika, nutmeg, cinnamon, cloves and ginger

Sauce

500 g (1 lb) tomatoes, finely chopped
1 small white onion, finely chopped
2 tablespoons finely chopped fresh parsley
1 clove garlic

1 cup water
paprika
¼ teaspoon cayenne pepper
salt

1   Combine meatball ingredients and mix well.
2   Roll into small balls and poach in boiling, salted water for 10 minutes, drain.
3   Simmer sauce ingredients together for 5 minutes.
4   Add kefta balls and simmer for ¼ hour.
5   Serve kefta balls in sauce.

Mongolian Lamb Curry

Serves: 4
Cooking time: 1¾ hours

1150 kJ (275 cal) per serve

1 large onion
1 large carrot
2 large cooking apples
3 cups water

½ teaspoon finely chopped green ginger
salt and pepper
3 teaspoons curry powder
500 g (1 lb) leg lamb, boned

Accompaniments

lemon wedges
tomato wedges
diced cucumber

½ cup drained pineapple pieces (fresh or unsweetened canned)

1   Roughly chop onion, carrot and one apple.
2   Place vegetables and apple in a saucepan with water, ginger, salt, pepper and curry powder. Bring to the boil, and simmer for 45 minutes to form a curry sauce.
3   Purée or blend curry sauce, return to the saucepan.
4   Remove all visible fat from lamb, cut into 2.5 cm (1 in) cubes.
5   Add lamb to sauce and simmer curry gently for 50 minutes.
6   Peel and dice remaining apple and add to lamb. Simmer for a further 10 minutes.
7   Serve with a tray of accompaniments.

Mongolian Lamb Curry

California Lamb Chops

Serves: 4
Cooking time: 40 minutes
Oven temperature: 180°C (350°F)

885 kJ (210 cal) per serve

750 g (1½ lb) chump lamb chops
juice of 1 lemon
½ cup syrup from peaches

2 tablespoons finely chopped fresh mint
1 cup artificially sweetened sliced
  peaches, drained

1 Trim all visible fat from chops.
2 Dry-fry chops until well browned on both sides, place in a flat baking dish.
3 Drain off remaining fat in the pan, add lemon juice and peach syrup. Boil rapidly until volume of sauce has been reduced by half. Add mint.
4 Pour sauce over chops, and top with peach slices. Bake for 30 minutes. Serve.

Lamb Chops in Cider

Serves: 4
Cooking time: 1½ hours
Oven temperature: 180°C (350°F)

1280 kJ (395 cal) per serve

750 g (1½ lb) chump lamb chops
1 large onion, finely sliced
2 large cooking apples

salt and pepper
2 cups dry apple cider

Garnish
2 tablespoons finely chopped fresh parsley

1 Dry-fry chops in a pan until well browned on both sides. Remove from the pan. Cook onions until soft.
2 Leaving skins of apples on, remove core and slice apples crosswise into approximately 6 thick slices each.
3 Layer chops, apples and onions in an ovenproof casserole, and sprinkle with salt and pepper.
4 Pour cider into the frying pan, simmer gently for 10 minutes, stirring frequently.
5 Add cider to casserole, and bake in the oven for 1 hour at 180°C (350°F).
6 Remove and serve garnished with parsley.

Turkish Kebabs

Serves: 4
Cooking time: 10-15 minutes

950 kJ (225 cal) per serve

Marinade
½ **cup dry sherry**
1 **clove garlic, crushed**
1 **small white onion, finely chopped**
2 **tablespoons finely chopped fresh parsley**

½ **teaspoon dried oregano**
salt
black pepper, freshly ground

Kebabs
500 g (1 lb) **leg lamb, boned**
1 **medium green pepper (capsicum)**
2 **medium tomatoes**

1 **large white onion**
1 **medium zucchini**
90 g (3 oz) **button mushrooms**

1 Combine marinade ingredients and mix well.
2 Trim all visible fat from meat and cut into 2.5 cm (1 in) cubes.
3 Place in marinade mixture and toss well.
4 Cover bowl and refrigerate for 12-24 hours, turning meat at intervals.
5 Cut green pepper (capsicum), tomato, onion and zucchini into 2.5 cm (1 in) cubes. Place meat on large metal skewers alternately with green pepper, tomato, onion, zucchini and mushrooms.
6 Brush meat and vegetables with marinade and cook over a barbecue or under a griller. Baste frequently.

Lamb Provencal

Serves: 8
Cooking time: 2 hours
Oven temperature: 180°C (350°F)

735 kJ (175 cal) per serve

1.5 kg (3 lb) **leg of lamb**
2 **cloves garlic, finely chopped**
4 **tablespoons finely chopped fresh parsley**
2 **chicken stock cubes**

3 **cups water**
salt
black pepper, freshly ground

1 Rub garlic and parsley over lamb, place on a rack in a baking dish.
2 Dissolve stock cubes in water and pour into the baking dish.
3 Season with salt and pepper.
4 Bake in the oven at 180°C (350°F) for about 2 hours or until cooked, turning and basting lamb at intervals.
5 If the pan becomes dry, add more water.
6 Slice meat, discarding any visible fat. Allow 125 g (4 oz) per serve.

Lamb Cutlets Lyon

Serves: 4
Cooking time: 8 minutes

545 kJ (130 cal) per serve

8 lamb cutlets
½ cup dry white wine
2 bay leaves

1 clove garlic, finely chopped
salt
black pepper, freshly ground

1 Trim all visible fat from cutlets and place cutlets in a shallow dish.
2 Mix wine, bay leaves, garlic, salt and pepper together and pour over the cutlets.
3 Marinate cutlets for approximately 4 hours, turning at intervals.
4 Remove cutlets and cook under a hot griller for approximately 8 minutes (4 minutes on each side) or until cooked.
5 At intervals during the cooking brush chops with the marinade.

Lamb Heléne

Serves: 4
Cooking time: 1 hour
Oven temperature: 180°C (350°F)

995 kJ (235 cal) per serve

500 g (1 lb) leg lamb, boned
1 tablespoon polyunsaturated oil
250 g (8 oz) mushrooms, peeled and sliced

½ cup dry vermouth
salt and pepper
2 tablespoons non-fat natural yoghurt

Garnish

parsley, chopped

1 Trim all visible fat from lamb. Cut meat into 2.5 cm (1 in) cubes.
2 Heat oil in a shallow pan, add lamb and fry for approximately 5 minutes.
3 Add mushrooms and cook a further 5 minutes. Add vermouth. Bring to the boil.
4 Place in an ovenproof casserole, season with salt and pepper, cover and bake until tender (approximately 40 minutes).
5 Remove from oven. Allow to cool for a few minutes.
6 Stir in yoghurt. Sprinkle with chopped parsley and serve.

Baked Lamb Chops

Serves: 4
Cooking time: 1-1¼ hours
Oven temperature: 190°C (375°F)

875 kJ (210 cal) per serve

8 chump lamb chops
1 large onion, sliced
2 cups canned peeled tomatoes
salt

black pepper, freshly ground
2 teaspoons finely chopped fresh mint
1 cup water

1 Trim all visible fat from chops. Place chops in a baking dish.
2 Combine onion, tomatoes, seasonings, mint and water. Pour over chops.
3 Bake in the oven at 190°C (375°F) for 1-1¼ hours.

Roast Lamb Creole

Serves: 8
Cooking time: 2 hours
Oven temperature: 180°C (350°F)

765 kJ (185 cal) per serve

1.5 kg (3 lb) leg spring lamb
½ cup unsweetened tomato juice
1 tablespoon tomato paste
10 drops Tabasco sauce
3 tablespoons vinegar

2 beef stock cubes
salt
pinch black pepper
1 small onion, finely chopped
4 cloves garlic, crushed

1   Trim visible fat from meat. Place in a deep pan or baking dish.
2   Mix all other ingredients together. Pour over meat and cover with plastic wrap.
3   Marinate overnight, or for 8 hours, turning meat occasionally.
4   Place meat in a baking dish. Pour marinade over.
5   Bake in the oven at 180°C (350°F) for two hours, basting occasionally.
6   Serve, allowing 125 g (4 oz) per person.

Lamb Shanks Jardinière

Serves: 4
Cooking time: 1½ hours

1490 kJ (355 cal) per serve

4 lamb shanks
1 tablespoon polyunsaturated oil
1 medium onion, roughly chopped
½ cup canned champignons, drained
    and sliced
2 cups canned tomatoes, roughly chopped

1 cup unsweetened tomato juice
salt and pepper
1 teaspoon chopped fresh sage
1 teaspoon chopped fresh oregano
½ teaspoon chopped fresh thyme
250 g (8 oz) green beans

Garnish

parsley, chopped

1   Remove skin and visible fat from meat. Heat oil in a frying pan and brown meat well. Remove meat and place in a heavy saucepan.
2   Fry onion and champignons and add to meat.
3   Add tomatoes, tomato juice, salt, pepper and herbs to the pan. Simmer for 5 minutes. Pour sauce over meat.
4   Cover meat and simmer gently for 1¼ hours.
5   String, top and tail beans, and slice thickly.
6   Add beans, cook for a further 10 minutes, then serve garnished with parsley.

Barbecued Loin of Lamb

Serves: 8
Cooking time: 50 minutes
Oven temperature: 160°C (325°F)

755 kJ (180 cal) per serve

1 **whole loin of lamb**	**salt**
2 **cloves garlic, finely chopped**	**black pepper, freshly ground**
¼ **cup soy sauce**	1 **tablespoon finely chopped fresh parsley**
½ **cup dry white wine**	2 **teaspoons finely chopped fresh mint**

1 Ask your butcher to trim loin and cut through the bone to form 1 piece of meat containing 16 chops.
2 Marinate loin in garlic, soy sauce, wine, salt, pepper, parsley and mint for at least 2 hours, turning and basting at intervals.
3 Place loin into an oven at 160°C (325°F) for approximately 40 minutes and then remove meat from the pan and barbecue over hot coals for a further 10 minutes, turning at intervals.
4 Cut into chops and trim all visible fat from meat before serving.

Lamb Chops Barossa

Serves: 4
Cooking time: 30 minutes

840 kJ (200 cal) per serve

750 **g (1½ lb) chump lamb chops**	3 **tablespoons red wine vinegar**
salt	10 **drops Tabasco sauce**
½ **cup chopped spring onions or shallots**	½ **teaspoon dry mustard**
4 **cloves garlic, crushed**	3 **tablespoons tomato paste**
salt and pepper	
125 **g (4 oz) fresh mushrooms, peeled and chopped**	

1 Trim all visible fat from chops. Place on a griller tray and sprinkle with salt.
2 Combine all other ingredients in a saucepan. Simmer for 10 minutes.
3 Spread half of the marinade over chops. Grill for 10 minutes.
4 Turn chops over, spread the remainder of the marinade on the other side. Grill for a further 10 minutes, or until cooked.

Stuffed Chump Chops

Serves: 4
Cooking time: 10 minutes

955 kJ (230 cal) per serve

4 **thick chump chops**	1 **tablespoon finely chopped fresh mint**
1 **medium onion, finely chopped**	**pinch mixed dried herbs**
2 **large mushrooms, finely chopped**	1 **tablespoon polyunsaturated margarine**
1 **medium tomato, finely chopped**	**salt and pepper**
1 **tablespoon finely chopped fresh parsley**	

1 Trim fat from chops and slit a pocket in each.
2 Mix remaining ingredients to make the stuffing.
3 Fill each pocket with stuffing and sew the edges together.
4 Place chops under a hot griller and cook for approximately 5 minutes on each side.

Spanish Lamb

Serves: 4
Cooking time: 1 hour
Oven temperature: 190°C (375°F)

805 kJ (190 cal) per serve

500 g (1 lb) lean leg lamb, boned
1 stalk celery, diced
1 medium onion, diced
1 tablespoon lemon juice
1 tablespoon tomato paste

1 teaspoon Worcestershire sauce
1 beef stock cube, crushed
1 cup water
salt and pepper
¼ teaspoon finely chopped fresh mint

1 Roll lamb and secure with string, place in a baking dish.
2 Combine celery, onion, lemon juice, tomato paste, Worcestershire sauce, stock cube, water, salt, pepper and mint. Spread over lamb.
3 Bake in the oven for 1 hour at 190°C (375°F), basting occasionally.
4 Remove meat and slice thinly.
5 Strain sauce from the pan, skimming off excess fat. Reheat.
6 Serve meat with accompanying sauce.

Lamb Chops Amandine

Serves: 4
Cooking time: 20 minutes

910 kJ (220 cal) per serve

4 double-thickness lamb chops
(middle loin)
1 medium onion, grated
1 small stalk celery, finely chopped
2 teaspoons finely chopped fresh parsley
½ teaspoon dried rosemary

rind of 1 lemon, grated
1 tablespoon lemon juice
1 tablespoon chopped toasted almonds
salt
black pepper, freshly ground

1 Trim chops well, leaving enough tail to wrap around chop.
2 Cut a pocket on the inside edge of each chop.
3 Mix all other ingredients together.
4 Stuff chops, and tie with cotton or secure with toothpicks.
5 Sprinkle with black pepper.
6 Cook under a hot griller for approximately 10 minutes on each side.

Loin Chops Lisbon

Serves: 4
Cooking time: 10 minutes

765 kJ (180 cal) per serve

8 middle loin lamb chops
4 tablespoons finely chopped fresh mint
½ cup lemon juice
1 teaspoon grated lemon rind

1 clove garlic, finely chopped
salt
black pepper, freshly ground

1 Trim all visible fat from the chops, and place chops in a shallow dish.
2 Mix mint, lemon juice, lemon rind, garlic, salt and pepper together, and pour over chops.
3 Marinate chops for approximately 4 hours, turning at intervals.
4 Remove chops and cook under a hot griller for 10 minutes (5 minutes on each side), or until cooked. Baste during cooking.

VEAL

Veal Coronet

Serves: 4
Cooking time: 30 minutes

1455 kJ (350 cal) per serve

750 g (1½ lb) sliced veal
3 teaspoons polyunsaturated oil
125 g (4 oz) fresh mushrooms, sliced
1 medium onion, sliced
1 clove garlic, crushed
1 bay leaf
1 tablespoon tomato paste

pinch dried oregano
2 sprigs each of thyme and parsley
1 chicken stock cube, crumbled
¼ cup red wine
¼ cup water
salt

1   Pound veal and cut into serving-size pieces.
2   Heat oil in a large flat pan and fry veal for 2 minutes on both sides.
3   Remove veal and add mushrooms and onions to the pan and toss over heat for 2 minutes.
4   Return veal to the pan and add garlic, bay leaf, tomato paste, oregano, thyme, parsley, stock cube, wine, water and salt.
5   Cover pan and simmer for 25 minutes or until tender.
6   Remove bay leaf, thyme and parsley sprigs and serve.

Blanquette de Veau

Serves: 4
Cooking time: 1 hour 45 minutes

1540 kJ (370 cal) per serve

750 g (1½ lb) stewing veal
1 cup water
2 chicken stock cubes
½ cup dry white wine
1 onion, roughly chopped
12 peppercorns
1 bay leaf
2 cloves garlic, crushed

salt
250 g (8 oz) mushrooms, peeled and chopped
8-12 baby onions
6 baby carrots, peeled and cut lengthwise
1 egg yolk
2 tablespoons non-fat natural yoghurt

Garnish
fresh parsley or dill, chopped

1   Remove any visible fat from meat. Cut meat into 5 cm (2 in) pieces.
2   Blanch veal by covering with water and bringing to the boil. Cook for 5 minutes and drain.
3   Add 1 cup water, stock cubes, wine, onion, peppercorns, bay leaf, garlic and salt to meat. Simmer for 1 hour in a covered saucepan.
4   Remove bay leaf, peppercorns, and as much onion as possible.
5   Add mushrooms, onions and carrots. Simmer for a further ½ hour.
6   Lift meat and vegetables out of sauce with a slotted spoon. Cover and keep hot.
7   Strain stock. Boil until reduced and thickened. Remove from heat.
8   Combine egg yolk and yoghurt. Beat together well with a fork.
9   Pour stock slowly into yoghurt mixture, beating well. Pour mixture over meat. Sprinkle with parsley to serve.

Blanquette de Veau

155

Veau Grand'Mère

Serves: 4
Cooking time: 1½ hours

1645 kJ (395 cal) per serve

750 g (1½ lb) stewing veal
1 tablespoon polyunsaturated oil
1 large onion, sliced
2 large cooking apples, chopped

2 beef stock cubes
1 cup water
salt and pepper

Garnish
parsley, chopped

1   Trim all visible fat from meat. Cut meat into 2.5 cm (1 in) pieces.
2   Heat oil in a heavy saucepan. Add veal and brown well. Add onion and apples and cook for a further 5 minutes.
3   Crumble beef stock cubes over meat. Add water, and salt and pepper to taste.
4   Bring to the boil, then cover and simmer gently until veal is tender. If there is too much cooking liquid, remove lid and boil rapidly for 5 minutes to reduce.
5   Check flavour, serve garnished with parsley.

Veal Toledo

Serves: 4
Cooking time: 12 minutes

1445 kJ (345 cal) per serve

750 g (1½ lb) sliced veal
2 teaspoons polyunsaturated oil
2 medium onions, grated
2 medium tomatoes, peeled, seeded and roughly chopped
1 tablespoon soy sauce

1 stock cube, crumbled
2 tablespoons water
pinch ground cloves
pinch ground nutmeg
salt

1   Pound veal and cut across the grain into thin strips, approximately 5 cm x 1 cm x 1 cm (2 in x ½ in x ½ in).
2   Heat oil in a large flat pan and sauté meat for 5 minutes.
3   Remove meat from pan and add onions, tomatoes, soy sauce, stock cube, water, cloves, nutmeg and salt.
4   Simmer for 5 minutes.
5   Return meat to the pan and simmer in the sauce for a further 2 minutes or until tender.

Veau au Vin Blanc

Serves: 8
Cooking time: 3 hours
Oven temperature: 150°C (300°F)

1430 kJ (340 cal) per serve

1.5 kg (3 lb) shoulder veal, boned, rolled and tied
2 large white onions
2 large carrots
2 cups peeled tomatoes
2 bay leaves
salt
black pepper, freshly ground
2 garlic cloves, finely chopped
4 large sprigs parsley
2 cups dry white wine

1 Place veal into a baking dish.
2 Peel and finely slice onions and carrots and place in the baking dish.
3 Add tomatoes, bay leaves, salt, pepper, garlic, parsley and wine.
4 Cover the baking dish with a lid or aluminium foil and bake in the oven for 2½ hours at 150°C (300°F).
5 Uncover and bake for a further ½ hour or until meat is tender.
6 Remove meat from the pan and keep warm.
7 Drain vegetables from the meat juice and skim the fat from the juices.
8 Moisten vegetables with some of the meat juices and purée in an electric blender or push them through a wire sieve.
9 Add sufficient juice to the vegetable purée to make a pouring sauce.
10 Reheat the sauce, slice the meat and serve together.

Veal Romanoff

Serves: 4
Cooking time: 30 minutes

1370 kJ (330 cal) per serve

750 g (1½ lb) veal, sliced thinly
250 g (8 oz) strawberries, washed and hulled (reserve 4 for garnish)
1 chicken stock cube
½ cup water
½ cup rosé
3 tablespoons non-fat natural yoghurt, stirred

Garnish
4 strawberries, sliced
4 mint sprigs

1 Remove any skin and fat from meat.
2 Slice strawberries, reserving 4 for garnish.
3 Add stock cube and water to frying pan. Bring to the boil and add meat, turning frequently to seal. Allow liquid to boil away. Brown meat.
4 Add rosé, cover and simmer gently for 15 minutes or until veal is tender.
5 Remove meat and keep hot on a covered serving dish.
6 Add sliced strawberries to juice. Turn off heat, add yoghurt and stir in well.
7 Serve meat with sauce spooned over. Garnish with strawberries and mint sprigs.

Veal Laresa

Serves: 4
Cooking time: 45 minutes–1 hour

1285 kJ (305 cal) per serve

750 g (1½ lb) buttock veal
salt
black pepper, freshly ground
3 teaspoons Worcestershire sauce

1 cup water
1 chicken stock cube
1 clove garlic, finely chopped
4 tablespoons buttermilk

Garnish
2 teaspoons finely chopped fresh chives

1 Remove all visible fat from veal. Cut veal into 2.5 cm (1 in) cubes.
2 Place meat in a saucepan and add salt, pepper, Worcestershire sauce, water, stock cube and garlic.
3 Bring to the boil, reduce the heat and simmer for 45 minutes–1 hour.
4 Place buttermilk in a bowl and gradually stir in the liquid from the saucepan.
5 Pour back over meat and serve immediately with a sprinkling of chives.
Note: The liquid should not be reboiled after buttermilk has been added.

Veal Birds

Serves: 4
Cooking time: 1 hour

1535 kJ (365 cal) per serve

750 g (1½ lb) veal, thinly sliced

Stuffing
125 g (4 oz) mushrooms
1 medium onion, finely chopped
1 stalk celery, finely chopped
2 tablespoons chopped fresh parsley
1 tablespoon chopped fresh chives
pinch dried sage, or ½ teaspoon chopped
  fresh sage
2 tablespoons non-fat natural yoghurt

pinch paprika
salt and pepper
1 tablespoon polyunsaturated oil
1 cup water
2 chicken stock cubes
½ cup dry white wine
2 tablespoons lemon juice

1 Pound veal steaks until thin.
2 Mix stuffing ingredients together. Spread mixture on each piece of veal and roll up. Secure with a thread or toothpicks.
3 Heat oil in a frying pan. Add meat and brown on all sides.
4 Place meat in a heavy saucepan.
5 Add water and stock cubes to the frying pan. Dissolve brownings. Add wine and lemon juice. Pour over veal and simmer until tender (about 45 minutes).
6 Lift veal rolls from the saucepan. Remove threads and keep veal hot on a serving dish.
7 Boil sauce until reduced and thickened. Pour over meat.

Turkish Steamed Veal

Serves: 8
Cooking time: 3 hours

1240 kJ (295 cal) per serve

1.5 kg (3 lb) shoulder veal, boned, rolled and tied
1 tablespoon coarse salt

Garnish
1 tablespoon table salt
1 teaspoon cumin

½ teaspoon cumin
pinch saffron, or ¼ teaspoon turmeric
black pepper, freshly ground

1 Rub meat with the salt, cumin, saffron or turmeric and pepper, and wrap in a clean kitchen towel.
2 Place into the top section of a large double steamer over boiling water. (The lower pan should be three-quarters full of water.)
3 Place a tightly fitting lid over the steamer and steam veal over a high heat for 3 hours without removing the lid.
4 Veal should be served accompanied by a bowl of mixed salt and cumin.

Vitello Tonnato

Serves: 6
Cooking time: 3 hours
Oven temperature: 180°C (350°F)

1405 kJ (335 cal) per serve

1 kg (2 lb) boned veal rump
salt
pepper
1 cup dry white wine
2 tablespoons chopped fresh parsley
2-3 fresh sage leaves, chopped

3 cloves garlic, cut into slivers
6 peppercorns
pinch ground dill
1 cup tinned red salmon, drained
juice of ½ lemon
1 egg yolk

Garnish
parsley, chopped

1 Trim all visible fat from meat. Sprinkle meat with salt and pepper. Place in a deep casserole. Add wine, parsley, sage, garlic, peppercorns and dill.
2 Remove bones and skin from salmon. Add flesh to the casserole, cover and cook in the oven for 1½ hours at 180°C (350°F). Remove from the oven and allow to cool.
3 Refrigerate meat. Purée cooking liquid and salmon in an electric blender or push firmly through a wire sieve. Add lemon juice. Bring to the boil, lower heat and simmer until reduced to half. Cool slightly.
4 Slice meat thinly. Arrange on an ovenproof serving dish. Cover and heat in the oven for about 25 minutes.
5 In the top of a double saucepan beat egg yolk, and then slowly blend in the salmon sauce. Stir until slightly thickened. Do not boil.
6 Remove meat from the oven and pour the sauce over the meat. Sprinkle with parsley and serve.

Ragoût of Veal

Serves: 4   *1610 kJ (385 cal) per serve*
Cooking time: 1 hour
Oven temperature: 180°C (350°F)

750 g (1½ lb) veal, thinly sliced
1 tablespoon polyunsaturated oil
2 small zucchini, sliced
salt and pepper

1 large tomato, sliced
1 medium onion, sliced
3 tablespoons tomato paste
½ cup water

1 Trim all visible fat from meat. Slice meat into strips and fry in oil until well browned.
2 Place zucchini slices in a casserole. Spoon meat over this and sprinkle with salt and pepper.
3 Lay tomato slices over meat. Top with onion slices. Sprinkle with salt and pepper.
4 Mix tomato paste with water. Pour into the casserole, cover and bake in the oven for 45 minutes at 180°C (350°F).

Veal Scallopini with Pineapple

Serves: 4   *1895 kJ (450 cal) per serve*
Cooking time: 20 minutes

750 g (1½ lb) veal, thinly sliced
1 tablespoon polyunsaturated oil
60 g (2 oz) blanched almonds, slivered
pepper and salt
1 large onion, sliced

½ teaspoon dry mustard
¼ teaspoon paprika
¼ cup dry sherry
2 tablespoons non-fat natural yoghurt

Garnish
½ cup drained unsweetened pineapple
  pieces

1 Trim all visible fat from meat. Heat oil in a frying pan. Add meat and almonds and brown. Sprinkle with pepper and salt.
2 Add onion and brown. Sprinkle with mustard and paprika. Pour sherry over and simmer for 5 minutes.
3 Remove meat from the pan and keep hot. Mix yoghurt into pan juices, spoon over meat and serve, accompanied by pineapple pieces.

Veal Gourmet

Serves: 4
Cooking time: 20 minutes
Oven temperature: 180°C (350°F)

1450 kJ (345 cal) per serve

8 veal cutlets, each weighing about
  90 g (3 oz)
90 g (3 oz) mushrooms, finely chopped
1 medium onion, finely chopped
2 tablespoons finely chopped fresh parsley

2 tablespoons finely chopped fresh chives
salt
black pepper, freshly ground
pinch mixed dried herbs
1 tablespoon polyunsaturated margarine

Garnish
4 sprigs parsley

1 Remove all visible fat from cutlets and pound cutlets until flat.
2 Place remaining ingredients in a bowl and mix well.
3 Spread this mixture over 4 cutlets and cover each with another cutlet. Press firmly together and wrap each pair of cutlets separately in aluminium foil.
4 Place in a shallow baking dish and bake in the oven at 180°C (350°F) for 20 minutes or until tender.
5 Remove foil, drain excess juice from cutlets and serve with a sprig of parsley.

Veal Palentino

Serves: 4
Cooking time: 15 minutes

1410 kJ (335 cal) per serve

750 g (1½ lb) veal cutlets
250 g (8 oz) mushrooms, sliced
salt
black pepper

1 tablespoon lemon juice
½ cup dry sherry
1½ cups asparagus spears
3 tablespoons non-fat natural yoghurt

Garnish
1 teaspoon finely chopped fresh parsley

1 Remove all visible fat from veal and pound into thin, flat steaks.
2 Place mushrooms, salt, pepper and lemon juice in a frying pan and cover with water.
3 Cover the pan and cook mushrooms until soft. Drain mushrooms and remove from the pan, retaining juices.
4 Add veal to the pan and seal quickly on both sides.
5 Pour off juices and retain.
6 Add sherry to the pan, ignite and allow to burn out.
7 Pour juices back into the pan, cover and cook veal until tender (about 8 minutes).
8 Return mushrooms to the pan and add asparagus spears and heat gently.
9 Drain juices from the pan.
10 Place yoghurt in a bowl and gradually stir in meat juices to make a creamy sauce.
11 Serve meat with asparagus and mushrooms.
12 Pour over sauce and sprinkle with chopped parsley.

Veal Piquant

Serves: 4
Cooking time: 20 minutes

1440 kJ (345 cal) per serve

4 veal steaks, each weighing about 185 g (6 oz)
2 teaspoons polyunsaturated margarine

1 tablespoon soy sauce
1 cup dry white wine
2 cups asparagus spears, drained

Garnish
parsley, chopped

1 Pound steaks until thin.
2 Melt margarine in a frying pan. Add meat, brown and cook through.
3 Remove and keep hot on a serving dish.
4 Add soy sauce and wine to the pan. Bring to the boil, add asparagus spears and simmer for 8 minutes.
5 Lift asparagus out of the pan and lay over meat. Keep hot.
6 Reduce sauce by boiling rapidly for 5 minutes. Spoon over meat and serve garnished with parsley.

Veal and Apple Curry

Serves: 4
Cooking time: 45 minutes–1 hour

1385 kJ (330 cal) per serve

750 g (1½ lb) topside or shoulder veal
2 medium cooking apples
1 medium onion
2 teaspoons curry powder
1 pinch chilli powder

1 clove garlic, crushed
1 beef stock cube
1 cup water
1 large bay leaf
salt

1 Trim veal of all visible fat. Cut veal into 4 cm (1½ in) cubes.
2 Peel, core and dice the apples.
3 Peel and slice the onion.
4 Place all ingredients into a saucepan, cover and bring to the boil.
5 Reduce heat and simmer for 45 minutes–1 hour.
6 Remove bay leaf and serve.

Veal Portuguese

Serves: 4
Cooking time: 2 hours
Oven temperature: 180°C (350°F)

1360 kJ (325 cal) per serve

750 g (1½ lb) veal buttock
2 cloves garlic
2 tablespoons tomato paste
10 drops Tabasco sauce
salt

black pepper
1 teaspoon Worcestershire sauce
2 tablespoons water
2 teaspoons polyunsaturated oil

1 Trim all visible fat from meat.
2 Cut garlic into fine slivers, and insert in tiny pockets on all sides of the meat.
3 Combine tomato paste, Tabasco sauce, salt, pepper and Worcestershire sauce with the water.
4 Place oil in a small baking dish. Add meat then spoon sauce over. Bake until meat is cooked. Slice and serve.

Veal Cutlets and Green Pepper Sauce

Serves: 4
Cooking time: 10 minutes

1435 kJ (340 cal) per serve

4 veal cutlets, each weighing 185 g (6 oz)
3 teaspoons polyunsaturated oil
1 cup water
1 tablespoon tomato paste

1 medium green pepper (capsicum), sliced
1 chicken stock cube
salt
1 tablespoon non-fat natural yoghurt

1 Pound veal.
2 Heat oil in a large flat pan, fry cutlets for 2 minutes on each side, and remove from the pan.
3 Add water and stir in meat juices.
4 Add tomato paste, green pepper (capsicum), stock cube, salt and meat.
5 Cover the pan and simmer for 6 minutes.
6 Drain off the juices and slowly add to yoghurt to make a creamy sauce.
7 Serve cutlets topped with green pepper (capsicum) and sauce.

Osso Bucco

Serves: 4
Cooking time: 1½ hours

900 kJ (215 cal) per serve

4 thick slices veal shins
salt
black pepper, freshly ground
1 clove garlic, finely chopped
1 medium onion, finely chopped

½ cup Chicken Stock (see page 45), or 1
  stock cube dissolved in ½ cup hot water
½ cup dry white wine
3 tablespoons tomato paste

Garnish
4 tablespoons finely chopped fresh parsley
rind of 1 lemon, finely grated

1 Place veal shins into a large saucepan and sprinkle with salt and pepper.
2 Add garlic and onion to meat.
3 Pour stock and wine over meat and stir in tomato paste.
4 Cover, bring to the boil, reduce heat and simmer for 1½ hours.
5 Serve, sprinkled with parsley and lemon rind.

Sweet and Sour Veal

Serves: 4
Cooking time: 35–45 minutes

1505 kJ (360 cal) per serve

750 g (1½ lb) topside or shoulder veal
1 medium green pepper (capsicum)
1 medium carrot
1 chicken stock cube
2 cups unsweetened pineapple pieces

1 tablespoon vinegar
1 teaspoon finely chopped green ginger
½ cup water
salt

1 Trim all visible fat from veal. Cut veal across the grain into thin strips approximately 5 cm x 1 cm x 1 cm (2 in x ½ in x ½ in).
2 Cut green pepper and carrot into thin strips.
3 Place all ingredients into a saucepan and bring to the boil.
4 Reduce heat and simmer gently for 35–45 minutes or until meat is tender.

Veal Piccata

Serves: 4
Cooking time: 45 minutes–1 hour

1355 kJ (325 cal) per serve

750 g (1½ lb) buttock veal
1 cup unsweetened tomato juice
1 medium onion, finely chopped
1 tablespoon paprika
salt

black pepper, freshly ground
½ teaspoon dried oregano
1 chicken stock cube
125 g (4 oz) mushrooms, sliced
1 medium green pepper (capsicum), sliced

1   Remove all visible fat from veal, and cut veal into 2.5 cm (1 in) cubes.
2   Place into a saucepan and add tomato juice, onion, paprika, salt, pepper, oregano and stock cube.
3   Bring to the boil and simmer for 35–45 minutes.
4   Add mushrooms and green pepper (capsicum) to meat.
5   Simmer for a further 10 minutes and serve.

Stuffed Veal Roast

Serves: 4
Cooking time: 2 hours
Oven temperature: 180°C (350°F)

1470 kJ (350 cal) per serve

750 g (1½ lb) veal buttock
1 cup drained unsweetened apricots

salt
1 tablespoon polyunsaturated oil

1   Trim all visible fat from meat. Cut a pocket in the side of meat.
2   Place apricots in the pocket and tie very securely.
3   Sprinkle meat with salt.
4   Place oil in a baking dish. Roll meat in oil. Bake in the oven at 180°C (350°F) for about 2 hours or until cooked. Remove the string. Slice the meat and serve hot or cold.

Veal Paprika

Serves: 4
Cooking time: 10 minutes

1355 kJ (325 cal) per serve

750 g (1½ lb) veal cutlets
2 teaspoons polyunsaturated oil
½ cup water
1 chicken stock cube

2 teaspoons paprika
salt
2 tablespoons non-fat natural yoghurt

Garnish
1 teaspoon finely chopped fresh parsley

1   Pound veal and cut into serving-size pieces.
2   Heat oil in a flat pan and fry meat for 2 minutes on either side.
3   Add water, chicken stock cube, paprika and salt, and simmer for 6 minutes or until tender.
4   Gradually drain juice from pan and stir into the yoghurt to make a creamy sauce.
5   Serve, sprinkled with parsley.

Veal Marengo

Serves: 4
Cooking time: 45 minutes–1 hour

1355 kJ (325 cal) per serve

750 g (1½ lb) topside or shoulder veal
1 medium onion, sliced
2 tablespoons tomato paste
2 large sprigs each of parsley and thyme
2 bay leaves
salt

black pepper, freshly ground
2 tablespoons lemon juice
1 teaspoon finely chopped green ginger
1 cup water
185 g (6 oz) mushrooms, sliced

1 Trim all visible fat from veal and cut into 4 cm (1½ in) cubes.
2 Place meat, onion, tomato paste, parsley, thyme, bay leaves, salt, pepper, lemon juice, ginger and water into a saucepan or flameproof casserole.
3 Cover, bring to the boil, reduce heat and simmer for 35–45 minutes.
4 Add mushrooms to saucepan and simmer for a further 10 minutes or until meat is tender.
5 Remove herbs and serve.

Veal and Plum Casserole

Serves: 4
Cooking time: 1 hour 15 minutes

1745 kJ (415 cal) per serve

250 g (8 oz) yellow plums
½ cup water
pinch cinnamon
artificial liquid sweetener
1 kg (2 lb) veal chops
1 tablespoon polyunsaturated oil

1 large cooking apple, peeled and cut
  into chunks
125 g (4 oz) potatoes, peeled and cut
  into chunks
salt and pepper
2 tablespoons dry vermouth

1 Cook plums in water until soft, and remove stones. Purée plums and liquid in an electric blender or rub through a sieve. Add cinnamon and enough sweetener to remove the sour taste from plums.
2 Trim visible fat from meat. Cut meat into 5 cm (2 in) pieces. Fry in oil until well browned. Remove and put in a saucepan.
3 Brown apple and potato. Add to meat. Sprinkle with salt and pepper.
4 Pour off any oil from the pan. Add plum sauce to pan and dissolve any brownings. Pour over meat. Add vermouth.
5 Cover and simmer for 1 hour. Serve.

DESSERTS

Australians consume about 49 kilograms (108 pounds) of sugar per person each year. Sugar contributes approximately 2,100 kilojoules (500 calories) extra to the average diet each day. Thus it is easy to see the connection between excess sugar in the diet and the problems of obesity and heart disease—two of Australia's major health problems.

When referring to sugar in the diet we are concerned not only with the amount you may add to your tea or coffee, but also with the 'hidden' sugar to be found in soft drinks, cordials, commercial cakes, pies and pre-sweetened cereals. Honey and raw sugar are two other sweetening agents which people use liberally, often without realising that these substances too are high in energy value, but low in nutritional value.

We have attempted to create desserts that do not include sugar, flour or cream. These recipes are, therefore, low in kilojoules (calories), saturated fats and cholesterol, and can be incorporated successfully in your diet.

- Many commercially prepared desserts, puddings and cakes are not only high in sugars and flours but also high in saturated fats and cholesterol. The wise shopper should avoid these products.
- The best desserts are those which consist of fresh fruits of the season. Who can resist a tempting fruit salad or gently poached fresh fruits?
- Chilled, non-fat natural yoghurt makes an excellent topping for fruits and desserts.
- When fresh fruits are not available, canned unsweetened or artificially sweetened fruits can be put to a variety of uses.
- Whipped Topping can be substituted for cream in many of your favourite recipes.
- Brazil nuts, cashew nuts, hazel nuts and peanuts are relatively low in saturated fat content and can all be used in combination with fruit and milk desserts. However, it is wise to remember that nuts have a high energy value, and if used indiscriminately can add to those excess kilojoules (calories).

Peach Coronets (page 172)

Bananas Caribbean

Serves: 4
Cooking time: 15 minutes
Oven temperature: 180°C (350°F)

525 kJ (125 cal) per serve

4 small bananas
rind and juice of 1 orange
rind and juice of ½ lemon
¼ cup unsweetened pineapple juice
pinch powdered cloves

pinch ground cinnamon
2 teaspoons polyunsaturated margarine
liquid artificial sweetener
2 tablespoons dark rum

1 Peel bananas and cut each in half lengthwise. Place in a baking dish.
2 Blend juices, spices and margarine in a saucepan. Bring to the boil and reduce to half the volume. Remove from stove, add sweetener to taste and pour over bananas.
3 Bake in the oven at 180°C (350°F) for about 10 minutes or until bananas are soft. Remove from oven.
4 Warm rum, pour over bananas and ignite. Serve immediately.

Cherries Jubilee

Serves: 4
Cooking time: 15 minutes

495 kJ (120 cal) per serve

250 g (8 oz) fresh cherries, stems removed
1 cup water
1 slice lemon
¼ teaspoon cinnamon

liquid artificial sweetener
4 tablespoons brandy
12 tablespoons Ice-cream (see page 188)

1 Place cherries in a saucepan with water, lemon slice and cinnamon. Simmer gently for 10 minutes and allow to cool.
2 Add artificial sweetener to taste.
3 Place cherries and liquid in a shallow pan or chafing dish. Pour brandy over cherries and ignite.
4 Spoon Ice-cream into serving dishes, add cherries and serve.

Peaches 'n' Cream

Serves: 4

520 kJ (125 cal) per serve

1 cup non-fat cottage cheese
4 passionfruit, pulp only
1 cup finely diced unsweetened pineapple
liquid artificial sweetener

2 drops yellow food colouring
4 artificially sweetened peach halves, drained
cinnamon

1 Blend cottage cheese until creamy and smooth with an electric beater or in a blender.
2 Add passionfruit pulp, pineapple, sweetener to taste and food colouring.
3 Spoon one-quarter of the mixture into each of 4 glass serving dishes. Place 1 drained peach half on each.
4 Sprinkle with cinnamon. Chill before serving.

Peaches Cardinal

Serves: 4   *190 kJ (45 cal) per serve*
Cooking time: 30 minutes

2 fresh peaches, peeled, halved and stoned
½ cup water
pinch cinnamon

2 tablespoons lemon juice
liquid artificial sweetener
1 cup fresh raspberries, rinsed and hulled

1 Poach peach halves gently in ½ cup water, flavoured with cinnamon and 1 tablespoon lemon juice. When cool, sweeten to taste.
2 Drain peaches and place in a bowl.
3 Purée raspberries in a blender or push through a sieve with a wooden spoon. Sweeten to taste and add remaining lemon juice.
4 Pour raspberry purée over peaches, cover and refrigerate for at least 3-4 hours, preferably overnight.
5 Place peach halves in 4 serving dishes. Spoon purée over the top.
6 The peaches may be served with Ice-cream (see page 188) or Whipped Topping (see page 188).

Marinated Kiwi Fruit

Serves: 4   *330 kJ (80 cal) per serve*

4 kiwi fruit (Chinese gooseberries)
pulp of 4 passionfruit
liquid artificial sweetener

¼ cup unsweetened pineapple juice
2 tablespoons rosé

1 Peel and slice kiwi fruit, place in a serving bowl.
2 Combine passionfruit pulp, artificial sweetener to taste, pineapple juice and rosé with kiwi fruit.
3 Cover and refrigerate for 1 hour before serving.

Marinated Fruit Skewers

Serves: 4   *510 kJ (120 cal) per serve*
Cooking time: 15 minutes

2 cups cubed fresh pineapple
1 banana, cut into thick slices
1 orange, cubed
1 kiwi fruit (Chinese gooseberry), cut into thick slices

12 whole strawberries, washed and hulled
1 cup unsweetened pineapple juice
1 teaspoon finely chopped green ginger
liquid artificial sweetener
8 skewers

1 Place fruit in a bowl.
2 Heat pineapple juice with ginger for 5 minutes. Remove from heat, discard ginger, and sweeten to taste.
3 Pour marinade over fruit and refrigerate for 1 hour.
4 Place pieces of fruit alternately on skewers, allowing 2 skewers per person. Place skewers on a flat dish and grill until fruit is lightly browned. Turn fruit and baste frequently with marinade. Serve hot.

Peach Coronets

Serves: 4
Cooking time: 30 minutes
Oven temperature: Peaches—180°C (350°F)
Meringue—230°C (450°F)

415 kJ (100 cal) per serve

6 artificially sweetened peach halves
30 g (1 oz) ground almonds
1 egg, white and yolk separated

1 teaspoon lemon juice
liquid artificial sweetener

1 Rub 2 peach halves through a sieve, or purée in a blender.
2 Place 4 peach halves in a baking dish with the hollow side up.
3 Mix peach purée, almonds, egg yolk, lemon juice and sweetener and spoon mixture into the cavities of the peaches. Bake in the oven at 180°C (350°F) for 20-25 minutes, or until mixture is firm and starting to turn golden. Remove from oven. Increase oven temperature to 230°C (450°F).
4 Beat egg white until stiff. Add artificial sweetener to taste and mix in well.
5 Pile egg white onto peaches. Cook quickly in the hot oven until the meringue is lightly browned. Serve hot.

English Fruit Compote

Serves: 4
Cooking time: 10 minutes

270 kJ (65 cal) per serve

1 small pear, peeled, cored and quartered
1 small apple, peeled, cored and cut into 8 wedges
4 yellow plums, cut into halves, stones removed
½ cup drained unsweetened canned pineapple

12 fresh, whole cherries
4 cloves
pinch cinnamon
½ cup water
liquid artificial sweetener

1 Place all the fruit in a saucepan, placing apples and pineapple at the bottom. Add spices and water.
2 Bring to the boil, reduce heat and simmer gently for 10 minutes until fruit is tender. Cool.
3 Place fruit in glass serving dishes, allowing 1 piece pear, 2 pieces apple, 2 plum halves, 3 cherries and 2 pieces pineapple per serve.
4 Sweeten syrup with artificial sweetener and spoon over the fruit. Refrigerate for 2 hours before serving.

Note: If fresh plums are unavailable, substitute tinned, artificially sweetened apricot or peach halves.

Sparkling Jellied Rhubarb

Serves: 6   *75 kJ (20 cal) per serve*
Cooking time: 15 minutes

375 g (12 oz) rhubarb
½ cup cold water
½ lemon, sliced
¼ teaspoon ground cinnamon
3 drops red food colouring

2 teaspoons gelatine
1 tablespoon warm water
liquid artificial sweetener
1 x 285 ml (10 fl. oz) bottle artificially
sweetened dry ginger ale

1   Wash rhubarb, remove all leaves and discard.
2   Slice rhubarb, and cook in the water with lemon slices and cinnamon until tender, but retaining its shape. Remove lemon slices. Allow rhubarb to cool. Add red food colouring.
3   Sprinkle gelatine over 1 tablespoon warm water, dissolve over hot water, then allow to cool slightly.
4   Add sweetener to rhubarb, then gelatine and dry ginger ale.
5   Pour mixture into a wet mould and set in the refrigerator until firm.
6   Turn out by plunging mould into boiling water for 5 seconds and inverting mould onto serving dish.

Brandied Orange Surprise

Serves: 4   *320 kJ (75 cal) per serve*
Cooking time: 10 minutes
Oven temperature: 180°C (350°F)

4 oranges
1 tablespoon brandy

liquid artificial sweetener
2 egg whites

1   Cut tops off oranges and scoop out the flesh.
2   Dice the orange flesh and mix with the brandy and sweeten according to taste.
3   Place mixture back into the orange shells.
4   Beat the egg whites stiffly and sweeten with artificial sweetener.
5   Spoon or pipe egg white over the fruit in the orange shells and bake for approximately 10 minutes at 180°C (350°F) or until the egg white is beginning to brown.
6   Serve immediately.

Oranges in Claret

Serves: 4   *380 kJ (90 cal) per serve*
Cooking time: 2 minutes

1 cup claret
¼ teaspoon ground cinnamon
4 oranges

liquid artificial sweetener
4 tablespoons Whipped Topping (see
page 188)

1   Place claret and cinnamon in a saucepan and bring to the boil.
2   Boil for 1 minute to evaporate the alcohol, then remove from heat.
3   Peel and thinly slice the oranges, removing all pith.
4   Pour the claret over the oranges and sweeten to taste with artificial sweetener.
5   Chill well and serve with Whipped Topping.

Blushing Apples

Serves: 4
Cooking time: 45 minutes

275 kJ (65 cal) per serve

4 cooking apples, peeled
12 drops red food colouring
2 cups dry cider

½ teaspoon ground cinnamon
pinch ground cloves
artificial sweetener

1 Place peeled apples in a saucepan.
2 Add half the red food colouring to the cider and pour over the apples. Add cinnamon and cloves.
3 Simmer gently in a covered saucepan until apples are soft, but not breaking up. Turn frequently so red colour is evenly absorbed.
4 When apples are tender, remove and place in serving dishes.
5 Reduce cooking liquid by boiling rapidly for 5 minutes until only half a cup remains. Add the remainder of the red colouring and sweeten to taste with artificial sweetener.
6 Spoon glaze over apples and serve either warm or chilled.

California Baked Apples

Serves: 4
Cooking time: 1 hour
Oven temperature: 180°C (350°F)

565 kJ (135 cal) per serve

4 cooking apples
2 cups orange juice
¼ teaspoon cinnamon

2 teaspoons polyunsaturated margarine
liquid artificial sweetener

1 Peel and core apples and place in a baking dish.
2 Heat orange juice in a saucepan. Add cinnamon and margarine. Bring to the boil and reduce to half the volume. Allow to cool slightly. Add sweetener to taste and pour over apples. Cover dish.
3 Bake at 180°C (350°F) for 45 minutes, basting frequently, or until apples are tender but not too soft.
4 Spoon sauce over the apples and serve. If sauce appears too thin, reduce by boiling rapidly for 5 minutes.

Strawberries Romanoff

Serves: 4

450 kJ (105 cal) per serve

2 cups strawberries
liquid artificial sweetener
juice and rind of 1 orange

1 tablespoon brandy
½ quantity Whipped Topping (see page 188)

1 Wash and hull berries. Place in a bowl and add artificial sweetener to taste.
2 Add orange juice and rind, and brandy. Chill in refrigerator.
3 Place 3 tablespoons Whipped Topping in each of the serving dishes. Spoon strawberries and juice over the top. Spoon remainder of topping over strawberries and serve.

Orange Cups

Serves: 4   *570 kJ (135 cal) per serve*

5 large oranges

Filling — 1st layer

1 cup non-fat cottage cheese   **pinch ground cinnamon**
liquid artificial sweetener   **2 teaspoons gelatine, dissolved in**
1 tablespoon lemon juice   **1 tablespoon hot water**
1 tablespoon brandy   **1 tablespoon orange juice**

Filling — 2nd layer

1 teaspoon gelatine, dissolved in   **liquid artificial sweetener**
  1 tablespoon hot water   **1 tablespoon brandy**
1 cup orange juice

Garnish
mint sprigs

1 Cut tops off 4 oranges. Scoop out pulp and set aside. Retain 1 tablespoon orange juice.
2 Peel the 5th orange and cut the flesh into small dice.
3 1st layer: Beat cottage cheese until creamy, then purée in a blender or push through a sieve to remove any lumps.
4 Add sweetener to taste, lemon juice, brandy, cinnamon and gelatine. Combine orange juice and pulp with cottage cheese mixture. Check flavour and add more sweetener if needed.
5 Divide equally into four portions and spoon into orange cases. Allow to set in the refrigerator.
6 2nd layer: Combine gelatine, orange juice, sweetener to taste and brandy. Spoon jelly over 1st layer in cases and set in the refrigerator.
7 When set, decorate with mint sprigs and serve.

Strawberry Flambé

Serves: 4   *280 kJ (65 cal) per serve*
Cooking time: 1-2 minutes

375 g (12 oz) strawberries, washed   **liquid artificial sweetener**
  and hulled   **4 tablespoons Whipped Topping (see**
2 tablespoons brandy   **page 188)**
⅓ cup unsweetened orange juice

1 Place strawberries in a chafing dish or frying pan, add brandy, bring to the boil and ignite.
2 Allow flame to burn out, add orange juice.
3 Remove from heat, allow liquid to cool slightly and add sweetener according to taste.
4 Serve either hot or chilled with Whipped Topping.

Burgundy Pears

Serves: 4
Cooking time: 1 hour

460 kJ (110 cal) per serve

4 fresh pears
8 whole cloves
1 cup burgundy
1 cup orange juice

½ teaspoon cinnamon
2 slices lemon
liquid artificial sweetener

1   Leaving stems intact, peel pears. Place whole pears upright in a saucepan. Pierce each pear with 2 cloves.
2   Add burgundy, orange juice, cinnamon and lemon slices to pan. Bring to the boil, reduce heat, and simmer gently for 45 minutes. Turn pears frequently to allow colour of wine to be absorbed evenly.
3   Remove cloves from pears. Place pears in individual serving dishes.
4   Boil cooking liquid rapidly until volume is reduced by half. Cool, add sweetener to taste, then pour over pears.
5   Serve warm or chilled.

Raspberry Mousse

Serves: 4

690 kJ (165 cal) per serve

1 cup fresh raspberries
¼ cup cold water
½ cup skim milk powder
2 teaspoons gelatine
½ cup boiling water

3 drops vanilla essence
3 drops raspberry essence
3 drops pink food colouring
1 egg white
liquid artificial sweetener

Garnish
2 tablespoons Whipped Topping (see page 188)
4 whole raspberries

1   Place raspberries, water and skim milk powder into a blender and purée.
2   Dissolve gelatine in boiling water, cool until mixture begins to set, add to raspberry mixture and whip with an electric beater until light and fluffy.
3   Add vanilla essence, raspberry essence and colouring.
4   Beat egg white separately until stiff.
5   Gradually fold the raspberry mixture into the egg white, using a metal spoon.
6   Sweeten to taste with artificial sweetener and pour into 4 individual glass dishes (each holding approximately ½ cup).
7   Put in the refrigerator to set.
8   Decorate with Whipped Topping and raspberries.

Yoghurt Custard

Serves: 4   *205 kJ (50 cal) per serve*
Cooking time: 20 minutes
Oven temperature: 150°C (300°F)

3 egg whites
1 cup skim milk
½ cup non-fat natural yoghurt
liquid artificial sweetener

3 drops yellow food colouring
3 drops vanilla essence
ground nutmeg

1 Beat egg whites gently. Add skim milk, yoghurt, sweetener to taste, yellow colouring and vanilla and beat together.
2 Pour into a small baking dish, stand this dish in a larger dish containing cold water. Sprinkle with ground nutmeg and bake in the oven at 150°C (300°F) for 20 minutes or until set.

Apple and Walnut Meringue

Serves: 4   *540 kJ (130 cal) per serve*
Cooking time: 20 minutes
Oven temperature: 180°C (350°F)

4 medium cooking apples
½ cup water
30 g (1 oz) walnuts, finely chopped

liquid artificial sweetener
4 egg whites

1 Peel, core and slice apples. Simmer in water until soft (5-10 minutes), and cool.
2 Stir walnuts through apples.
3 Sweeten to taste with artificial sweetener and transfer to 4 small individual ovenproof dishes.
4 Beat egg whites until stiff and sweeten to taste with artificial sweetener.
5 Spread the meringue mixture evenly over the apple.
6 Bake in the oven at 180°C (350°F) for 10 minutes or until meringue is golden brown.

Almond Surprise

Serves: 4   *345 kJ (85 cal) per serve*
Cooking time: 5 minutes

4 artificially sweetened pear halves
1¼ cups skim milk
½ teaspoon almond essence
2 drops red food colouring

liquid artificial sweetener
2 junket tablets
1 tablespoon warm water

Garnish
1 tablespoon almond flakes

1 Slice pears (half per person) and place in individual serving dishes.
2 Warm milk to blood heat.
3 Add essence, food colouring and artificial sweetener to taste.
4 Crush junket tablets in 1 tablespoon warm water. Pour milk over mixture and blend lightly. Pour over pears in dishes.
5 Sprinkle almonds over pears. Allow to set, then chill in refrigerator.

Coffee Carumba

Serves: 4   *1200 kJ (285 cal) per serve*

1 tablespoon instant coffee powder
2 cups non-fat natural yoghurt
½ cup walnuts, chopped

½ teaspoon liquid artificial sweetener
½ teaspoon vanilla essence

Garnish
2 tablespoons Whipped Topping (see page 188)
4 whole walnut kernels

1   Place coffee in large mixing bowl and blend with 1 tablespoon of the yoghurt.
2   Add remaining yoghurt, walnuts, sweetener and vanilla. Mix well.
3   Spoon mixture into 4 ½-cup moulds and place in the freezer to set.
4   Remove from freezer 20 minutes prior to serving to soften.
5   Turn out mould by plunging quickly into boiling water and inverting onto a serving plate.
6   Garnish each dessert with 2 teaspoons of Whipped Topping and a walnut kernel.

Golden Pudding

Serves: 4   *760 kJ (180 cal) per serve*
Cooking time: 20 minutes

180 g (6 oz) pumpkin, peeled and cut into pieces
½ teaspoon ground cinnamon
pinch ground nutmeg
pinch ground mixed spice
½ cup drained and puréed unsweetened peaches

grated rind and juice of 1 lemon
liquid artificial sweetener
90 g (3 oz) walnuts, chopped
2 level teaspoons gelatine
1 tablespoon warm water
1 egg white

1   Cook pumpkin in boiling water until tender. Drain off liquid and mash pumpkin well. If lumpy, purée in a blender or rub through a sieve.
2   Add spices, peach purée, lemon juice and artificial sweetener to taste. Add walnuts.
3   Sprinkle gelatine over 1 tablespoon warm water. Dissolve over hot water. Cool slightly, then fold into mixture.
4   Beat egg white until soft peaks form. Fold into pumpkin. Spoon into 4 serving dishes.
5   Refrigerate until set.

Summer Salad

Serves: 4   *420 kJ (100 cal) per serve*

1 orange
1 kiwi fruit (Chinese gooseberry)
½ cup unsweetened canned pineapple
2 passionfruit

1 banana
12 strawberries
½ cup unsweetened orange juice
1 tablespoon dark rum

1   Peel orange, remove pips, cut flesh into dice.
2   Peel kiwi fruit, cut into slices, then cut each slice in half.
3   Scoop out pulp of passionfruit.
4   Slice banana.
5   Wash and hull strawberries.
6   Mix all fruit gently together, add orange juice and rum, and chill well prior to serving.

Floating Islands

Serves: 4   *220 kJ (50 cal) per serve*
Cooking time: 15 minutes

1 egg white
liquid artificial sweetener
1¼ cups skim milk
1 egg
3 drops vanilla essence

3 drops yellow food colouring
rind of 1 orange, grated
1 tablespoon orange juice
liquid artificial sweetener

1   Beat egg white and artificial sweetener to taste, until stiff peaks form. Divide into four portions.
2   Warm milk over a low heat. When hot, but not boiling, add half the beaten egg white in 2 spoonfuls. Poach each side for 1-2 minutes. When the egg white is set, remove to a plate and cook the remaining 2 spoonfuls. Lift out onto a plate.
3   Beat egg, vanilla essence, food colouring, orange rind and juice, and sweetener to taste.
4   Gradually add the hot milk to the egg mixture, beating with a wooden spoon. Pour mixture back into the saucepan.
5   Cook over a pan of simmering water, stirring constantly, until custard just coats the spoon. Pour custard into serving dishes. Place one meringue on each serve of custard.
6   Serve warm or chilled.

Cassata Royale

Serves: 8   *685 kJ (165 cal) per serve*

1 quantity Ice-cream (see page 188)
½ teaspoon almond essence
1 tablespoon rum
½ cup strawberries, washed, hulled and chopped
½ cup drained and chopped unsweetened pineapple pieces

3 drops red food colouring
2 teaspoons instant coffee, dissolved in 1 teaspoon cold water
30 g (1 oz) blanched, slivered almonds
30 g (1 oz) walnuts, chopped

1   Divide Ice-cream into three equal portions.
2   Blend almond essence into one-third of Ice-cream and spoon into a 1-litre (2-pint) mould or basin. Place in freezer until it begins to set.
3   Combine rum, strawberries, pineapple and red colouring with one-third of Ice-cream mixture. Spoon this fruit mixture into mould to form second layer.
4   With the remaining portion of Ice-cream, combine the coffee, almonds and walnuts. Add this final layer to the mould.
5   Refrigerate overnight or until quite firm.
6   To serve, plunge mould into boiling water for 5 seconds, remove and invert onto a serving platter.
7   Cut into 8 equal wedges.

Cheesecake

Serves: 8   *635 kJ (150 cal) per serve*
Cooking time: Crust—10 minutes
*   Filling—45 minutes*
Oven temperature: 180°C (350°F)

Crust
⅓ cup ground almonds
6 starch-reduced crispbread, finely crushed

10 drops artificial sweetener
2 tablespoons polyunsaturated margarine, melted

Filling
500 g (1 lb) non-fat cottage cheese
1 egg

grated rind and juice of 2 lemons
½ teaspoon liquid artificial sweetener

Garnish
nutmeg, grated

1   Mix crust ingredients together. Spoon mixture into the base of a 20 cm (8 in) pie dish, reserving 2 tablespoons for decoration. Press down firmly over the base and partly up the sides of the dish.
2   Bake for approximately 10 minutes, then allow to cool.
3   Place cottage cheese in a mixing bowl, and beat to a creamy consistency with an electric beater. Sieve to remove any lumps.
4   Beat egg slightly and add to cheese.
5   Add lemon rind and strained juice, and sweetener. Mix well together and pour over crumb base. Sprinkle with nutmeg and decorate edges with remaining crust mixture.
6   Bake in the oven at 180°C (350°F) for 45 minutes, or until set.
7   Allow to cool, then chill in refrigerator.
8   Divide into 8 wedges and serve.

Cheesecake

Bombe Alaska

Serves: 6
Cooking time: 5 minutes
Oven temperature: 250°C (475°F)

775 kJ (185 cal) per serve

1 quantity Ice-cream (see page 188)
1 cup puréed strawberries

3 egg whites
liquid artificial sweetener

Garnish
6 strawberries, hulled and quartered
1 tablespoon brandy

1   Spoon Ice-cream into a 1-litre (2-pint) basin lined with plastic wrap, and freeze.
2   When Ice-cream is set, turn out onto a flat oven-tray by plunging basin into boiling water for 5 seconds. Remove plastic and refreeze quickly. Cover Ice-cream with strawberry purée. Return to freezer to harden.
3   Beat the egg whites until stiff and sweeten to taste with artificial sweetener.
4   Spread egg whites over entire surface of Ice-cream. With a spoon make a well in the top of the meringue.
5   Bake dessert in the oven at 250°C (475°F) for 5 minutes or until meringue is just beginning to brown. Remove quickly.
6   Decorate with quartered strawberries.
7   Heat brandy, ignite and pour carefully into the well formed in the meringue.
8   Serve while still flaming. Cut into wedges.
Note: Avoid pouring brandy over the sides of the meringue, or the heat of the flame will burn the meringue.

Cantaloup Berry Frappé

Serves: 4

440 kJ (105 cal) per serve

2 cups cantaloup (rock melon) pulp
2 cups blackberries, washed and stems removed
½ cup unsweetened orange juice

1 tablespoon lemon juice
liquid artificial sweetener
Whipped Topping (see page 188)

1   Place cantaloup pulp, blackberries, orange juice and lemon juice and purée in a blender (or use an electric beater).
2   Add artificial sweetener to taste, pour into a freezer tray. Freeze until mixture is beginning to set.
3   When purée appears mushy, remove from freezer and beat or whip for 5 minutes. Return to freezer and set.
4   Fifteen minutes before serving, remove from freezer. This will allow frappé to soften a little. Divide equally into four serves and pile into glass dishes.
5   Serve with Whipped Topping.
Note: Fresh raspberries or strawberries may be substituted for blackberries.

Bombe Alaska

Ice-cream

Serves: 12   *340 kJ (80 cal) per serve*

2 cups cold water
250 g (8 oz) skim milk powder
1 tablespoon vanilla essence
2 teaspoons liquid artificial sweetener

4 drops yellow food colouring
2 teaspoons gelatine
1 tablespoon warm water

1 Add skim milk powder to cold water. Beat until powder is dissolved.
2 Add vanilla, sweetener and food colouring.
3 Sprinkle gelatine over 1 tablespoon warm water. Stand over hot water until melted. Cool slightly.
4 Add gelatine to milk, then beat with electric beater on high speed until creamy.
5 Pour into a dish and place in freezer. When Ice-cream begins to set, remove from freezer. Beat mixture again until thick and creamy.
6 Return to freezer to set.
7 Allow 3 rounded tablespoons per serve.

Whipped Topping

Yield: 2 cups   *135 kJ (30 cal) per rounded tablespoon*

125 g (4 oz) skim milk powder
¾ cup water

½ teaspoon vanilla essence
liquid artificial sweetener

1 Add milk powder to water in a large mixing bowl.
2 Add vanilla and sweetener to taste.
3 Beat with an electric beater until the mixture is very thick and creamy.
4 Cover and chill in the refrigerator until required.

Cairns Cooler (page 194)

BEVERAGES

Whether you require a thirst-quenching long drink or an aromatic hot toddy, we hope you will gather ideas from the recipes in this section for a drink with a difference!

These recipes have been written particularly for people who have been advised to limit their alcohol intake.

- In several recipes you will find instructions to quickly boil wine or spirits. The purpose of this is to evaporate the alcohol (and consequently reduce the number of kilojoules or calories), while retaining the characteristic flavour of the wine.
- Artificially sweetened tonic water, dry ginger ale, bitter lemon and lemonade can be used freely in cocktails, long drinks and fruit punches as they contain few kilojoules (calories).
- Whipped Topping may be used to replace cream in hot beverages.
- Buttermilk and yoghurts can be blended with fresh fruit juices to make a nutritious between-meal drink.

Foreground: *Coffee Kosciusko (page 196);* left: *Strawberry Granita (page 192);* right: *Lemon Swirl (page 194)*

Ginger Mint

Serves: 4   *225 kJ (55 cal) per serve*

2 cups unsweetened orange juice
4 large sprigs mint

2 x 285 ml (10 fl. oz) bottles artificially
sweetened dry ginger ale

Garnish
4 ice-blocks
4 sprigs mint

1   Pour orange juice into a jug.
2   Slightly crush mint, combine with orange juice and refrigerate for at least 2 hours.
3   Remove mint and pour orange juice into 4 chilled, long glasses.
4   Top each glass with chilled dry ginger ale, an ice-block and mint. Allow 250 ml (8 fl. oz) per person.

Sangria Tertulia

Serves: 4   *20 kJ (5 cal) per serve*
Cooking time: 1 minute

2 cups claret
½ cup water
1 lemon, thinly sliced

1 orange, thinly sliced
liquid artificial sweetener

Garnish
8 ice-blocks
4 orange slices

1   Place the claret and water into a saucepan, bring to the boil and simmer for 30 seconds.
2   Pour over the lemon and orange slices and marinate in the refrigerator for 4 hours.
3   Strain the marinade, sweeten to taste with artificial sweetener and serve with two ice-blocks and an orange slice. Allow 125 ml (4 fl. oz) per serve.

Strawberry Granita

Serves: 4   *75 kJ (20 cal) per serve*

20 medium strawberries
1½ cups cracked ice

2 x 280 ml (10 fl. oz) bottles artificially
sweetened tonic water

1   Wash and hull the strawberries.
2   Place strawberries, ice and ½ bottle of tonic water into a blender. Mix at a high speed for 30 seconds.
3   Pour into 4 long glasses and top each glass with tonic water. Allow 250 ml (8 fl. oz) per person.

Spiced Tomato Juice

Serves: 4   *120 kJ (30 cal) per serve*

2 cups unsweetened tomato juice
1 teaspoon Worcestershire sauce
salt and pepper

squeeze lemon juice
liquid artificial sweetener
4 sprigs mint, crushed

Garnish

4 lemon slices

1 Combine all ingredients except garnish in a jug.
2 Refrigerate for 2 hours, remove mint.
3 Serve garnished with lemon slice.

Cucumber Refresher

Serves: 4   *105 kJ (25 cal) per serve*

1 small cucumber
½ medium green pepper (capsicum)
¼ medium white onion
2 chicken stock cubes

1 cup unsweetened tomato juice
1 tablespoon lemon juice
salt

1 Peel and roughly chop cucumber, green pepper and onion.
2 Place cucumber, green pepper, onion, stock cubes, tomato juice and lemon juice into a blender.
3 Liquify on a high speed, strain, add salt to taste and serve chilled.

Hawiewa Cocktail

Serves: 4   *175 kJ (40 cal) per serve*

1 cup unsweetened tomato juice
1 cup unsweetened pineapple juice
1 large sprig mint

Garnish
4 ice-blocks
4 small sprigs mint

1 Combine all ingredients except garnish and stand in a refrigerator for at least 1 hour to infuse.
2 Remove and discard mint.
3 Serve chilled with ice and topped with a small sprig of mint.

Apricot Fizz

Serves: 4   *260 kJ (60 cal) per serve*

200 g (7 oz) unsweetened apricot pieces
½ cup unsweetened orange juice
4 tablespoons Ice-cream (see page 188)

2 x 285 ml (10 fl. oz) bottles artificially sweetened lemonade, chilled

Garnish
4 sprigs mint

1   Place apricots and orange juice into a blender and reduce to a liquid.
2   Place 1 tablespoon of Ice-cream into each glass.
3   Pour equal quantities of fruit mixture into each glass and top with lemonade.
4   Serve immediately in long, chilled glasses garnished with mint. Allow 250 ml (8 fl. oz) per person.

Cairns Cooler

Serves: 4   *295 kJ (70 cal) per serve*

1 cup unsweetened orange juice
½ cup unsweetened pineapple juice
½ cup unsweetened grapefruit juice
4 strawberries, washed, hulled and halved
4 slices lemon
4 slices orange

4 slivers cucumber skin
1 x 285 ml (10 fl. oz) bottle artificially sweetened tonic water
1 x 285 ml (10 fl. oz) bottle artificially sweetened lemonade
crushed ice

1   Mix fruit juices, add strawberries, lemon and orange slices and cucumber skin.
2   Chill thoroughly, pour over crushed ice, top with tonic water and lemonade, and serve. Allow 250 ml (8 fl. oz) per person.

Lemon Swirl

Serves: 4   *120 kJ (30 cal) per serve*

1 cup lemon juice
1 cup unsweetened orange juice
liquid artificial sweetener

2 x 285 ml (10 fl. oz) bottles artificially sweetened bitter lemon

Garnish
4 swirls of lemon peel

1   Mix lemon and orange juice together and sweeten to taste with artificial sweetener.
2   Pour into an ice-block tray and place in freezer until the mixture is just set.
3   Crush the ice-blocks and place into 4 chilled, long glasses.
4   Top each glass with artificially sweetened bitter lemon and serve garnished with lemon peel.

Orange Buttermilk

Serves: 4   *335 kJ (80 cal) per serve*

2 cups buttermilk
2 cups unsweetened orange juice
liquid artificial sweetener

Garnish
4 ice-blocks
4 slices orange

1 Pour buttermilk into a jug.
2 Slowly add orange juice, stirring continually.
3 Add sweetener according to taste, and chill.
4 Pour into long glasses and add an ice-block and slice of orange to each glass. Allow 250 ml (8 fl. oz) per person.

Hot Cinnamon Toddy

Serves: 4   *5 kJ (1 cal) per serve*
Cooking time: 1 minute

1½ cups whiskey or brandy   **1 cinnamon stick**
4 strips of lemon peel   **1 cup water**
4 cloves   **liquid artificial sweetener**

1 Place whiskey or brandy into a saucepan with the lemon peel, cloves, cinnamon and water.
2 Bring to the boil and simmer for 30 seconds.
3 Strain the liquid, cool slightly, add artificial sweetener to taste and serve while still hot. Allow 125 ml (4 fl. oz) per person.

Café Royale

Serves: 4   *5 kJ (1 cal) per serve*
Cooking time: 1 minute

½ **cup brandy**
2 **strips of lemon peel**
2 **strips of orange peel**
1 **cinnamon stick**

2 **cups fresh black coffee, hot**
liquid artificial sweetener

1   Place brandy, lemon peel, orange peel and cinnamon into a saucepan.
2   Boil for 30 seconds.
3   Strain equal quantities into 4 cups and top with coffee.
4   Sweeten to taste with artificial sweetener. Allow 125 ml (4 fl. oz) per person.

Irish Coffee

Serves: 4   *135 kJ (30 cal) per serve*
Cooking time: 1 minute

½ **cup whiskey**
2 **cups black coffee, hot**
liquid artificial sweetener

4 **rounded tablespoons Whipped**
Topping (see page 188)

1   Pour whiskey into a saucepan, bring to the boil and simmer for 30 seconds.
2   Pour equal quantities into 4 cups and add black coffee.
3   Sweeten to taste with artificial sweetener and carefully top each cup with Whipped Topping.

Coffee Kosciusko

Serves: 4   *340 kJ (80 cal) per serve*

4 **teaspoons powdered instant coffee**
2 **tablespoons hot water**
4 **cups liquid skim milk, chilled**

1-2 **drops vanilla essence**
liquid artificial sweetener
4 **tablespoons Ice-cream (see page 188)**

Garnish
ground nutmeg

1   Place powdered instant coffee in a jug, add hot water and dissolve coffee.
2   Add skim milk and flavour to taste with vanilla essence and artificial sweetener. Refrigerate for 2 hours.
3   Pour into 4 long glasses.
4   Top each glass with Ice-cream and garnish with a sprinkling of nutmeg. Allow 250 ml (8 fl. oz) per serve.

Hot Claret Punch

Serves: 4
Cooking time: 1 minute

30 kJ (5 cal) per serve

1½ cups claret
3 tablespoons water
3 tablespoons unsweetened orange juice

2 tablespoons brandy
liquid artificial sweetener

Garnish
ground nutmeg

1 Place the claret, water, orange juice and brandy into a saucepan.
2 Bring to the boil and simmer for 30 seconds.
3 Sweeten to taste with artificial sweetener and serve hot with a sprinkling of nutmeg. Allow 125 ml (4 fl. oz) per person.

APPENDIX

DEFINITIONS

Fats in food

Fat is one of man's three main foods—the others being carbohydrate and protein—and in affluent western society, fat provides about 40% of the body's calories.

Although fat in the diet can take many forms, the differences in appearance, consistency and taste are due to relatively minor variations in chemical make-up. The great bulk of fat in food is made up of 'triglycerides'. There are three types of fats: saturated, monounsaturated and polyunsaturated.

Fats which are mostly saturated are usually solid: butter, lard and the fat on meat are examples and they come mostly from animals. Fats containing mainly polyunsaturated fatty acids are usually oily or liquid, such as safflower, sunflower or maize oil, and derive mainly from vegetable sources. There are, however, some exceptions to this rule.

The average Australian diet, which includes a mixture of fats (such as butter, meat fats, vegetable oils, milk and chocolate), contains about five times more saturated fat than polyunsaturated fat. It is said to have a P/S ratio of about 0.2.

The terms 'saturated' and 'polyunsaturated' have come into prominence in recent years in relation to diet and coronary heart disease, the link being another fatty substance, cholesterol, which is also found in food and in the body.

Cholesterol

Cholesterol is a normal and essential material in the human body. It is a chemical substance, one of the family of fats or lipids, as they are known technically. It is closely related chemically to many of the body's hormones and to the bile, and is found in all body cells and in the blood.

Some of the cholesterol in the body comes from our food and the rest is produced mainly in the liver. It is conveyed to all parts of the body by the bloodstream.

The concentration of cholesterol in the blood is usually consistent, but the level may vary either because of variations in production of cholesterol within the body, excretion of cholesterol from the body or through changes in the food intake. Some individuals build up high levels of cholesterol easily, and others tend to have low levels of cholesterol. In both cases, however, the levels will vary according to diet and other factors such as illness, body-weight changes, physical activity and drugs.

A test of blood cholesterol can be arranged by any doctor. It involves taking a small quantity of blood from a vein in the arm.

Cholesterol is one of the fatty substances which collect on the linings of the arteries, giving rise to the condition known as atherosclerosis. If the build-up of cholesterol reaches serious proportions in the coronary arteries, it leads to coronary heart disease—the commonest cause of death in adults of all ages in Australia. Coronary heart disease can take the form of either angina pectoris (recurring chest pains) or myocardial infarction (heart attack).

High levels of blood cholesterol are strongly associated with a high risk of coronary heart disease. There is evidence that high levels of cholesterol and other fats in the blood do, in fact, *cause* atherosclerosis and coronary heart disease, and that reduction of the level of fats reduces the risk of these conditions.

Blood cholesterol levels can be reduced within a few weeks by reducing the total amount of fat in the diet, by replacing saturated fats with polyunsaturated fats, and by avoiding foods with a high cholesterol content.

Triglyceride

Also linked with coronary heart disease, triglyceride forms the major part of animal and plant fat stores and thus the fats and oils in food. It is also the main fat, as we know it, in the human body. It is made up of 'building blocks' of fatty acids which consist of combinations of carbon, hydrogen and oxygen atoms.

The body stores of triglyceride come mainly from food, but some triglyceride is produced in the liver and other organs from carbohydrates (sugars, starches, etc.). Triglyceride is also carried from one part of the body to another in the bloodstream.

Studies have shown that people with high levels of triglyceride in the blood also have a high risk of coronary heart disease.

Triglyceride levels, like cholesterol levels, can be reduced by changes in diet. These mainly involve reduction of the total amount of food eaten, particularly fat, carbohydrates and alcohol, and reduction of excess weight.

ENERGY VALUES OF FOODS

One of our main purposes in producing this book is to show that tempting gourmet cooking is still possible while producing dishes which have a reduced kilojoule (calorie) and saturated fat content. We have, therefore, calculated the energy value per serve for each recipe.

What is a kilojoule?

Doctors, physiologists, scientists and engineers, in measuring the amount of energy or work that our body or any other machine expends, use various types of units. The units differ from one country to another and from one scientific field to another: they include calories, ergs, joules, kilojoules, and food poundals.

Nutritionists could measure the amount of energy or work provided by a given type or amount of food in any of these units, but it has been customary to use calories. By international agreement, however, from January 7, 1977, the unit used to measure work or energy is the kilojoule (kJ).

One calorie is equivalent to approximately 4 kilojoules (the exact value is 4.186). Thus, for instance, one gram of carbohydrate will provide approximately 4 calories or 16 kilojoules and a 30-minute walk requires 300 calories or 1200 kilojoules.

Three references were used to calculate the energy values of each recipe. For those wanting further information we suggest you use these books.

S. Thomas & M. Corden, *Tables of Composition of Australian Foods.* Commonwealth Department of Health, Australian Government Publishing Service. 1970.

B. Watt & A. Merrill, *Composition of Foods.* Agriculture Handbook No.8, United States Department of Agriculture. 1975.

U.S. Department of Health, Education and Welfare. *Food Composition Table for Use in East Asia.* Public Health Service, National Institute of Health. 1972.

To illustrate the energy values of some of the more common foods in your diet, the following table gives the kilojoule and calorie values for average serves.

APPROXIMATE ENERGY VALUES OF FOODS

ITEM	SERVING*	ENERGY VALUES**	
		kilojoules	calories
BREAD			
Brown	1 slice (35 g)	250	60
White	1 slice (23 g)	250	60
Wholemeal	1 slice (32 g)	305	70
Rolls, starch reduced	1 whole	105	25
Crispbread, starch reduced	1 biscuit	115	30
CEREALS			
Branflakes	1 cup	465	110
Cornflakes	1 cup	420	100
Wheatflake biscuits	2 biscuits	505	120
EGGS			
Whole	one (45 g)	300	75
White	one (289 g)	60	15
Yolk	one (17 g)	250	60
FATS AND OILS			
Butter	1 tablespoon	140	35
Margarine, polyunsaturated	1 teaspoon	140	35
Oil, polyunsaturated	1 tablespoon	705	170
FISH			
Pan-fried in 1 teaspoon margarine	1 fillet (100 g)	565	135
Poached, or baked with no fat	1 fillet (100 g)	425	100
Salmon, canned	½ metric cup	820	195
Tuna, canned in brine	½ metric cup	475	115
FRUITS			
Apple	1 small (100 g)	225	55
Apricots	3 whole (100 g)	190	45
Banana	1 medium (100 g)	365	90
Cantaloup (rock melon)	½ melon (120 g)	125	30
Grapefruit	½ grapefruit (120 g)	185	45
Orange	1 medium (130 g)	215	50
Orange juice	½ cup (250 ml)	210	50
Peach	1 medium (110 g)	185	45
Pear	1 medium (150 g)	350	85
Pineapple	1 slice (80 g)	175	40
Strawberries	12-14 whole (110 g)	95	20
MEATS			
Bacon, lean, grilled	2 strips (30 g)	835	200
Beef, fillet, grilled	130 g	2065	495
rump, grilled	130 g	1825	435
sirloin, grilled	100 g	1275	305
sirloin, roast	1 slice (75 g)	495	170
Chicken, breast, boiled	115 g	955	230
roasted	2 slices (75 g)	630	150

ITEM	SERVING*	ENERGY VALUES**	
		kilojoules	calories
Ham, lean, leg	2 slices (60 g)	985	235
Lamb, chops, chump	1 average (110 g)	1605	390
chops, loin	2 average (130 g)	1980	475
Pork, chop, grilled	1 medium (80 g)	1465	350
Veal, chop, grilled	1 average (75 g)	650	155
cutlets, grilled	100 g	1035	250
MILK AND MILK PRODUCTS			
Milk, skimmed	1 cup	340	80
whole	1 cup	710	170
Yoghurt, non-fat natural	1 cup	500	120
Cottage cheese, uncreamed	100 g	380	90
VEGETABLES			
Asparagus, canned	3 medium spears	45	10
Beans, green, boiled	½ cup	80	20
Broccoli, boiled	⅓ cup	55	15
Cabbage, raw	⅓ cup	40	10
Carrot, cooked	½ cup (90 g)	105	25
raw	1 small (60 g)	90	20
Cauliflower, boiled	½ cup	65	15
Corn, boiled	½ cup	240	60
Mushroom, sautéed in margarine	6-7 whole	275	65
Parsnip, boiled	⅓ cup	150	35
Peas, boiled	⅓ cup	180	45
Potato, boiled	1 medium	300	75
mashed	⅓ cup	185	45
Pumpkin, boiled	¼ cup mashed	80	20
Silverbeet (spinach) boiled	⅓ cup	75	20
ALCOHOL			
Beer	300 ml	500	120
Champagne	150 ml	525	125
Port	60 ml	355	85
Sherry (dry)	60 ml	295	70
Spirits	30 ml	294	70
Wine (dry)	150 ml	545	130
Wine (sweet)	150 ml	565	135

* Metric cup, tablespoon or teaspoon are the standard measures

** Energy contents are rounded to the nearest fifth kilojoule or calorie

INDEX

Page numbers in *italic* refer to illustrations